CENTRAL AMERICA AND UNITED STATES POLICIES, 1820s–1980s

Guides to Contemporary Issues
Richard Dean Burns, Editor

This series has been developed, in part, in cooperation with the Center for the Study of Armament and Disarmament, California State University, Los Angeles.

CENTRAL AMERICA AND UNITED STATES POLICIES, 1820s—1980s

A Guide to Issues and References

THOMAS M. LEONARD

Regina Books
Claremont, California

Library of Congress Cataloging in Publication Data

Leonard, Thomas M., 1937-
   Central America and United States policies, 1820s-1980s.

   (Guides to contemporary issues ; #4)
   Bibliography: p.
   Includes index.
   1. Central America — Foreign relations — United States.
   2. United States — Foreign relations — Central America.
   3. Central America — History — 1821-1951. 4. Central
America — History 1951-   . I. Title.   II. Series.
F1436.8.U6L46   1985   327.72073   85-1765

ISBN 0-941690-14-8
ISBN 0-941690-13-x (pbk.)

Cover Design by Clinton Wade Graphic Design

Regina Books
P.O. Box 280
Claremont, CA 91711
Manufactured in the United States of America

Preface

The turmoil in contemporary Central America threatens to destroy established economic, political, and social structures and, in fact, has done so in Nicaragua. For United States foreign policy, the turmoil presents new challenges because U.S. policymakers have long ignored the internal dynamics of Central American life.

This survey seeks to place the problems of the region and their implications for U.S. foreign policy in historical perspective. The first chapter reviews Central American history, emphasizing the emergence of an elite that controlled each nation's economic and political apparatus and enjoyed social privilege, all at the expense of the middle sector and lower socioeconomic groups. Toward the end of World War II these last two groups began to press their demands for change, which finally erupted into the violence of the 1970s and 1980s.

The second chapter traces the evolution of U.S. foreign policy toward Central America, by focusing on two fundamental objectives: (1) keeping Europeans out of the region and (2) maintaining order and stability. In so doing the United States accepted the ruling elite in each nation and ignored the demands and needs of middle sector and lower socioeconomic groups. When violence erupted in the 1970s, the United States appeared to be basing its policies and hopes on the old order.

The literature on Central America is vast. The selected bibliography emphasizes the most important works in English. Although the content of many works overlap national histories, time periods, and domestic and foreign policy, the bibliography's division parallels, as closely as possible, the sequence of events and issues in Chapters I and II.

I am indebted to many individuals for their assistance. Librarians Bruce Latimer, at the University of North Florida, and Mary Gormly and Professor Timothy Fox Harding at California State University, Los Angeles, generously gave their time. Suggestions from Thomas M. Campbell, Professor of History at Florida State University, Alfonso Chardy of the *Miami Herald's* Washington Bureau, and Roger R. Trask of the Defense Department's Historical Office, proved most valuable in completing the final draft. Laurrie Hurst Leonard patiently typed and retyped the manuscript. The continued encouragement from Richard Dean Burns guided this project to its completion.

Thomas M. Leonard

For

Tom, Bob, Randy,
Dave, Eddie, Stacy

Contents

Maps

Tables

Chart

I

Central America: Its Crisis
in Historical Perspective

The most obvious development in Central America's history was the concentration of political and economic power in the hands of a few. Spanish rule set the pattern for what followed. All authority and decisions were issued from a small ruling class with little opportunity for political participation by the great majority of inhabitants. Independence from Spain did not bring either constitutional government or economic prosperity. Politically, Spain was replaced by a new aristocracy and economically by other foreign markets.

The region's economic system reinforced the political system. Coffee replaced dyes following independence, and bananas replaced coffee in the twentieth century as the region's major industry. Subsequently, sugar, cotton, timber, and tobacco were commercially developed. Most agricultural production was for export and dependent on a large unskilled labor force. These agricultural operations contributed to a wide dichotomy in living standards between the landowners and the work force, a dichotomy that remains to the present. The banana industry brought in foreign capital; like the native landowners, these foreign interests wanted political tranquility to ensure the security of their investments. Foreign capital also developed the region's infrastructure, which in turn produced a middle sector, an amorphus group that enjoyed relative affluence, but lacked political participation. In each nation rural and urban unskilled labor historically remained outside the social and political apparatus. Attempts to improve the living standards of these groups after 1920 were branded communistic.

The middle sector and the lower socioeconomic groups came to be described as the generation of rising expectations by the end of World War II. The middle sector sought constitutional and democratic government, and the lower classes improved living standards.

Slowly after 1945 these groups challenged the established order and contributed to the contemporary crisis.

Developments to 1945

The Impact of Spanish Autocracy: The Colonial Heritage

The Spanish conquest of Central America was complete by 1545, but the administrative structure was not finalized until 1570 with the establishment of the Kingdom of Guatemala, an *audencia* within the Viceroyalty of New Spain. The Viceroyalty included all Spanish claimed territory in North America south to the isthmus of Panama, and eastward to the Caribbean islands. The Guatemalan *audencia* stretched from Chiapas in southwestern Mexico to Costa Rica. Guatemala emerged as the most important province in the *audencia.* Centralized authority was the most common characteristic. From the capital, at Guatemala City, authority flowed downward to the *corregidore* (magistrate) that administered each Indian village and to the *cabildo* (town council) in the larger cities. The town councils provided the local elite an opportunity to participate in politics and subvert Spanish authority. Because the principal settlements were located on the western side of the isthmus, cut off from the east by the high mountains and tropical jungles, Spanish dependence on her subjects' loyalty soon broke down. Both the *cabildos* and *hacendados* (large plantation owners) acted with great independence.

A monoculture, with all its trappings, developed. The *hacienda* produced staple crops for export—indigo, cocoa, and cattle—but was dependent on food imports. Fluctuation of world market prices and competition from other supply sources contributed to the emergence of a debtor-creditor relationship. Lacking the natural wealth of Mexico and Peru, and an adequate transportation system, Central America became an outpost in the Spanish American empire.

A rigid social structure further militated against a progressive society. In 1810, on the eve of independence, there were approximately 1.5 million inhabitants in the region, but only 100,000 were white. About 900,000 were pure Indians, about half as many were *mestizos* (Spanish-Indian mixed blood), and another 20,000 blacks and mulattoes. Only in Costa Rica did the whites outnumber the other racial groups. At the apex of the social structure were the *peninsulares,* administrators who came from Spain. Next came the *criollos,* also of pure Spanish blood, but who were born in the New World. Many *criollos* became *hacendados,* enjoying economic and social privilege; but found themselves politically second class citizens permitted to participate only in the *cabildos*. The mixed-blood *mestizos* were ignored by their pure blooded relatives, while Indians, blacks and mulattoes were reduced to forced labor, debt peonage, and in some cases slavery. The Roman Catholic Church became entrenched in Central America, as it was elsewhere in the Spanish empire. Although the Church had responsibility for education, vital statistics, and some social services, its fundamental concerns were in meeting spiritual needs. A significant aspect of the Church's influence in Central America was its tacit, if not open, support of the rigid class structure that evolved.

Patterns established during Central America's colonial period remained an important component of the region's history well into the twentieth century. The questions of restricted political participation and central authority dominated Central America's political history. Dependence on a single agricultural product and foreign investment plagued the region's economic development. A rigid class structure, reinforced by church authorities, prevented social mobility.

Government by the Elite: Liberals vs. Conservatives

Central America was not affected by Napoleon's imposition of French authority over Spain in 1810, which ignited independence movements elsewhere in Latin America. Not until the Spanish constitution of 1820 did the majority of Central America's politically articulate population seriously consider independence. That document, which provided for less central authority and greater civil liberties such as free press and speech, shocked Central American conservatives and made them less averse to breaking away provided they could maintain their privileged status. The document also encouraged the region's liberals, who opposed the central authority at Guatemala City and the primacy of the Church. Thus, for their own reasons, both liberals and conservatives supported the declaration of independence on September 21, 1821.

Following a tenuous union with Mexico that lasted only thirteen months the liberals seized the initiative, dominating a constituent assembly that convened in June 1823 and produced a federal constitution sixteen months later. Only Chiapas chose to remain with Mexico. Considered a compromise document, the constitution established the United Provinces of Central America and provided for a president and a congress to sit at Guatemala City, with state governments in each of the five provinces. Limited suffrage and a cumbersome indirect voting procedure facilitated the maintenance of power by the wealthier class. Catholicism became the official religion, and black slavery, never important, was abolished. The document reflected the colonial experience, except that it eliminated the Spanish *peninsulares* and slavery. In 1825, José Manuel Arce became the first president of the United Provinces of Central America.

Liberal-Conservative strife soon followed, paralyzing both the national congress and federal authorities. Civil uprisings began in 1826. Honduran liberal Francisco Morazán suppressed the revolts and a year later he was elected president of the union. Liberals also gained control of the state governments. Morazán won reelection in 1834, but his liberal policies contributed to the disintegration of the union. Church privileges were attacked with the introduction of religious toleration, civil marriage and trial by jury. The liberals also favored free trade, economic liberalization and republicanism. Opposing most of these reforms the conservatives favored the continuance of orthodox economic policies, strong central government and the maintenance of Church privileges. Conservatives were further infuriated by Morazán's effort to encourage immigration as a spur to economic development. In 1838, the national congress dissolved after declaring the provinces free to adopt any form of government they desired. Morazán's military effort to re-unite the empire failed and he was driven into exile. The provinces became the five independent nations of Central America.

Importantly, the liberal-conservative political rivalry formed during this federal period remained after the union's dissolution. Well into the twentieth century, wars erupted between the Central American nations simply because administrations of one political viewpoint were supportive of revolutionary movements against governments of a different political opinion. The political histories of El Salvador, Guatemala, Honduras, and Nicaragua were clearly connected, with Guatemala exercising great influence over the others. Largely due to its geographic isolation, Costa Rica managed to avoid the disorders that plagued the other four countries.

For approximately 55 years following the collapse of the confederation, there were two clearly defined periods in Central American history, both dominated by the Guatemalan political leadership. Rafael Carrera and the conservatives shaped the first, while Justo Rufino Barrios and the liberals molded the second. Carrera, who rose from obscurity to drive Morazán from Central America, remained the power behind conservative rule in Guatemala until 1854 when he made himself president. He governed as dictator until his death in 1865. During those years the conservatives and their clerical allies set out to restore the past. They reinstated the privileged position of the Church and invited the Jesuits and other religious orders to return.

Not satisfied with their position at home, the Guatemalans successfully restored conservative governments in El Salvador, Honduras and Nicaragua, but not without liberal resistance. The strongest resistence was encountered in Nicaragua. Liberal exiles journeyed to California to purchase arms and supplies, and enlist foreign recruits. Commanded by William Walker, these soldiers of fortune poured into Nicaragua, ousting the conservatives in 1855. Walker had himself "elected" president. In so doing however, he gave the Central Americans reason to forget their squabbles and unite to drive him from power. In 1860 Walker renewed his efforts to establish a self-proclaimed empire, but he was captured and executed before a Honduran firing squad. The defeat of the filibuster temporarily secured the conservative governments in all five countries. Unrest continued into the 1860s, however, and Carrera's army found it necessary to suppress Indian and *mestizo* rebellions at home and interfere in El Salvador and Honduras on behalf of conservatives.

With Carrera's death in April 1865, the political pendulum swung back to the liberals. Armed with new weapons—Winchester and Remington repeating rifles—the liberals attacked conservative strongholds in Guatemala, culminating in the fall of Guatemala City on June 20, 1871 to liberals Justo Rufino Barrios and Miguel García Granados. Although conservative resistance continued until 1874, the liberal attack on the landed aristocracy and the Church was immediate. Jesuits were again exiled, religious groups disbanded, property confiscated and leaders banished from Guatemala.

Like the conservative Carrera before him, Barrios was determined to install similar governments in the nations around him, and thus interfered in El Salvador and Honduras to effect the installation of liberal-minded executives. Affairs in Guatemala and these two nations kept Barrios fully occupied and unable to pursue liberal interests in Nicaragua or Costa Rica.

──────────── CHART I ────────────

Major Political Figures

United Provinces of Central America 1823-1828
Francisco Morazán (Honduras) 1826-1838

The Liberal-Conservative Struggle and the Search for Unity 1838-1930

Rafael Carrera (Guatemala) 1838-1865
Justo Rufino Barrios (Guatemala) 1873-1885
Tomás Guardia (Costa Rica) 1870-1882
José Santos Zelaya (Nicaragua) 1894-1909
Francisco Bertrand (Honduras) 1913-1919

The Age of the Dictators 1931-1956

Maximiliano Hernández Martínez (El Salvador) 1931-1944
Jorge Ubico (Guatemala) 1931-1944
Tiburcio Carías (Honduras) 1933-1949
Anastasio Somoza García (Nicaragua) 1936-1956

Post World War II 1945-1984

Juan José Arévalo (Guatemala) 1945-1950
José Figueres (Costa Rica) 1948-1958
Jacobo Arbenz Guzmán (Guatemala) 1951-1954
Anastasio Somoza Debayle (Nicaragua) 1956-1979
José Napoleon Duarte (El Salvador) 1972-1984
Fernando Romero Lucas Garcí (Guatemala) 1978-1982
Roberto Suazo Cordova (Honduras) 1982-1984

In early 1885 the political climate appeared to favor another effort at union. Barrios was determined to consolidate Central America under a liberal regime. The presidents of El Salvador and Honduras, Rafael Zaldívar and Luis Bográn, respectively, were placed in power by Barrios. A liberal, Próspero Fernández, governed in Costa Rica, and moderate conservative Evaristo Carazo in Nicaragua. When Barrios announced his plan in February 1885, however, vested and national interests rose in opposition. Only Honduran President Bográn approved the unification scheme. Undeterred, Barrios set out to impose unity. He marched his army into El Salvador, only to be killed in the first battle. With his death, the project collapsed.

Costa Rica remained relatively aloof from the region's political intrigues, but did follow the pattern of liberal development. In 1870, liberal Tomás Guardia seized power and immediately set out to crush the small oligarchical group that had ruled Costa Rica since independence. He expropriated their lands and divided them among the small landowners. Family rule followed for twenty years, as Guardia was succeeded by his brother-in-law Próspero Fernández, who in turn was succeeded by a relative of both, Bernardo Soto. In 1889, Soto permitted the first free and honest elections in the country's history, thus embarking Costa Rica on a history of democratic process. Political power, however, still remained in the hands of the upper class.

While the importance of liberalism to Central American politics dwindled following Barrios' death in 1885, the rivalry continued between the liberals and conservatives in each of the five states. The issue of union reappeared after 1893 when José Santos Zelaya seized power from the conservatives in Nicaragua. For the next sixteen years Zelaya replaced Barrios as the region's president-maker. Like Barrios, Zelaya interfered in the internal affairs of neighbor states in an effort to surround himself with men of similar views. In 1893 Zelaya helped to install Policarpo Bonilla in Honduras and in 1894 Rafael Gutiérrez in El Salvador, thus entrenching liberal leadership in three states. Zelaya's prestige was further enhanced by Nicaragua's annexation in 1895 of the Mosquito Coast (named after Indian residents of the region), which Britain had administered since 1848. With a sympathetic Guatemala, the time appeared proper to again attempt union. Only Costa Rica, which remained under conservative leadership in the 1890s, remained aloof from the scheme.

Zelaya's popularity enabled him to organize the Greater Republic of Central America, a loose confederation including Nicaragua, Honduras and El Salvador. The confederation lasted from 1895 to 1898. Like its predecessors in 1844 and 1851, the Republic suffered because the signatory states were not interested in granting the central government effective authority and support, and because Costa Rica and Guatemala refused to join. With the overthrow of El Salvador's Gutiérrez in 1898, the union disintegrated.

In 1902 Zelaya again called for establishment of a union, inviting his fellow presidents to a conference in Corinto. Only Guatemala refused to participate because its president, Manuel Cabrera, himself had visions of regional leadership. The other four presidents, however, agreed to a treaty calling for the settling of disputes through a regional tribunal, an important precedent for the next two decades.   A year later war threatened Central America as Cabrera and Salvadoran President Tomás Regaldo engaged in typical *caudillo* rivalry. Hostilities were delayed until 1906, when Regaldo encouraged Guatemalan emigrés in the other four countries to oust Cabrera. Regaldo lost his life, creating a power vacuum in El Salvador that Zelaya wanted to fill.

Also in 1903, conservative Manuel Bonilla seized control of the Honduran government, an act threatening both Zelaya's control in Nicaragua and his plans for union. The tense situation climaxed in 1906 when Honduran rebels, with Zelaya's blessing invaded Honduras and ousted Bonilla. Violation of Nicaragua's border by Honduran troops provided Zelaya the excuse to send his army into Honduras and install Miguel Dávila as president. To halt the spread of *Zelayista* influence, Guatemala's Cabrera and El Salvador's Fernando Figuerora joined forces. Hostilities ended thanks to a Mexican—United States peace initiative which resulted in the 1907 Washington Conference. Mexico had historic interests in Central America and also supported U. S. security objectives in the region. The episode is important because it marked a turning point in United States policy toward Central America—from one of relative indifference to one of involvement. For the next generation the United States became an integral part of Central American political dynamics.

From 1907 until 1920 there were no international conflicts in Central America, but internal political turmoil continued, notably in Nicaragua. In 1909 a revolution ousted Zelaya, and a brief civil war in 1912 resulted in the election of conservative Adolfo Díaz and, in 1916, of Emiliano Chamorro, also a conservative. Honduras was plagued by internal strife until 1913 when Francisco Bertrand became president. Cabrera successfully suppressed opposition in Guatemala. With the exception of the assassination of President Manuel Araujo in 1913, the notable Salvadoran landowning families of Menéndez and Quinones, by agreement, kept the conservatives in the presidential palace. In Costa Rica, the democratic process was interrupted by Federico Tinoco, who seized and held power from 1917 until 1919.

Regional stability ended with government changes in Honduras, El Salvador, Nicaragua and Costa Rica in 1919 and Guatemala in 1920. For the next thirteen years political turmoil plagued Central America. Only Costa Rica, returning to her traditional policy of isolation, avoided controversy.

The center of controversy became Honduras, where President Carlos Lagos permitted liberal exiles to gather, with the usual implications of organized revolts against their conservative home governments. He also persuaded Guatemalan President José Manuel Orellana, in May 1922, to join in a secret pact for a common defense against conservative enemies. This placed the governments in Tegulcigapa and Guatemala City against those in San Salvador and Managua. Border clashes soon followed, eventually resulting in the *Tacoma* agreement, a United States initiated peace pact. At the insistence of the United States, the *Tacoma* agreement also provided for the convening of a general Central American conference.

From December 1922 to February 23, 1923 representatives of the Central American states met in Washington, D.C., ultimately reaching several agreements designed to bring political stability to the region and to foster greater cooperation. Politically the most important agreement was that providing for nonrecognition of governments that came to power through a coup d'etat or revolution, unless legitimized by election. The election, however, could not sanction a rebel leader or close relative. Furthermore, the governments agreed not to encourage revolutionary activities within their borders or otherwise interfere in the internal affairs of their neighbor states. These treaty provisions soon came into play, but those concerning potential union—commissions to deal with customs, currency, banking, agriculture, elections—were never applied.

From 1923 to 1932 only Costa Rica avoided the political intrigue that affected application of the 1923 treaty. Honduras was first, when, in the 1923 presidential elections, Tuburcio Carías won a plurality, but not a clear majority, of the popular vote, and the Honduran congress could not muster a quorum to decide the issue. Carías took to the hills, declared himself president and began a revolution in 1924. He finally withdrew, however, when advised that recognition would not be granted his government according to the 1923 treaty. New elections were held in 1924, in which conservative Miguel Paz Barahona ran unchallenged; for the next eight years Honduras enjoyed political tranquility.

In Nicaragua liberal Carlos Solórzano won the fraudulent 1924 election only to be forcibly ousted two years later by conservative Emiliano Chamorro, who failed to gain recognition in accordance with the 1923 treaty provisions. Increasingly isolated, Chamorro stepped aside in favor of fellow conservative Adolfo Díaz, who gained recognition from the conservative Honduran and Salvadoran governments, but not the liberal regime in Guatemala. The United States subsequently intervened to supervise Nicaragua's 1928 election, which was won by liberal José Maria Moncada. Constitutional order was restored.

In December 1930, Guatemalan General Manuel Orellana engineered a coup in violation of the 1923 treaties. Orellana's Central American neighbors denied him recognition, and he subsequently was persuaded to resign. Free elections followed in February 1934. Unopposed, Jorge Ubico captured the presidency and embarked on a ten year dictatorship.

Two years later General Maximiliano Hernández Martínez engineered a coup in El Salvador. In violation of the 1923 treaty, he was denied recognition, but successfully weathered the crisis, ruling until his overthrow in 1944.

The 1923 treaties and subsequent events provided a watershed in Central American politics. The treaties mark the last effort at political union and their renunciation in 1934 signaled the beginning of dictatorships—Ubico in Guatemala, Hernández in El Salvador, Carías in Honduras and Anastasio Somoza in Nicaragua. Each governed with an iron hand, eliminating opposition through intimidation, exile, or jail. They remained in power through constitutional manipulations and/or fraudulent elections. The military became an important prop in each regime. Only Costa Rica avoided dictatorship, but political affairs there remained the domain of the wealthy class.

Central American politics since colonial days had been a privilege of the upper class. Independence only eliminated the Spanish *peninsulares*. Until the emergence of dictators in the 1930s political struggles were confined to the local landowning classes. During the 1930s the military's role in politics increased, except in Costa Rica. Outside the political process were the middle sector, and urban and rural labor groups. The latter constituted the largest single component of the sociopolitical structure. The middle sector and urban labor groups developed in the twentieth century and subsequently became the first initiators of political reform.

The Disparity of Wealth: Economic and Social Developments

Central America's climate and soil encouraged agricultural enterprises dating to colonial days. In the 1830s Costa Rica began coffee production, which by 1900 had become the chief export of all the Central American countries except Honduras. Coffee production permitted each nation to modernize, with Costa Rica leading the way. Government policies—tax relief, subsidies, transportation development, provisions for cheap land and labor—encouraged this expansion. Conservatives began these policies and after 1871 the liberals continued them. This helped explain the emergence of a new group of elite landowners in the latter part of the nineteenth century, and contributed to the liberal—conservative political struggle for the sixty years after 1871.

The liberals continued to advocate laissez-faire economic policies and anti-clericalism, but now that they controlled the government machinery they were willing to postpone democratic practices. After 1871 liberals were influenced by the philosophy of positivism, which emphasized material progress and scientific development. Application of liberal policies resulted in the imitation of northern European and United States values, the encouragement of foreign capital investment and the continuing insensitivity to working class needs.

With the exception of Church privileges, conservatives came to accept many positivist ideas, making the liberal-conservative political struggle from 1871 to 1930 little more than the "outs" wanting "in."

The primary export market for coffee came to be the United States. While coffee *fincas* remained in native hands, foreigners were permitted to participate and they soon melted into the local social structure. Liberals, aware of the dangers of a single product economy, encouraged expansion into sugar, cotton, cocoa, and timber. Gold in Nicaragua and silver in Honduras also became important exports, but coffee remained paramount. On the eve of World War I, coffee accounted for 85% of Guatemala's exports, 80% of El Salvador's, 63% of Nicaragua's and 35% of Costa Rica's.

The liberals also sought expansion of the transportation industry and commerce, but lacking native capital and foreign investments transportion expansion was very slow and manufacturing production was insufficient to meet domestic needs. Each nation was blessed with a favorable trade balance, but because the local elite preferred to invest their profits abroad, free from political insecurity and with a promise of greater return, Central American trade was controlled by foreign firms from the United States, Britain, Germany, and France.

Commercial expansion brought an increase in foreign goods, but their distribution was confined to the upper class.

As exports increased and commerce expanded, the Central American nations, with Costa Rica leading the way, undertook the modernization of their capital cities, except Tegulcigalpa, Honduras. Streets were paved, public parks, stadiums, buildings, and aqueducts were built; national theaters, libraries, museums, professional schools, and universities were established. Emphasis was on scientific and technical skills at the expense of the humanities and arts; there was no appreciation of native Indian cultures. Costa Rica proved the only exception, increasing its literacy rate from 11% in 1864 to 31% in 1892.

The liberals attacked the Church, a source of conservative strength, by stripping it of its lands, and nationalizing its endowments. The state took control of education, hospitals, charity, care for the aged and orphans—all formerly administered by the Church—and greatly restricted the public activities of its clerics. Although the conservatives remained loyal to the Church, its influence over the masses decreased.

The liberals also introduced a degree of professionalism to the military, particularly the officer corps. They established national military schools and brought in foreign instructors. Rank remained with the privileged, as few persons of the lower class were allowed to rise to higher officer positions. The military became the defender of the liberal governments, and often the arbiter and destroyer of government itself. Only service on the public debt outranked military expenditures in all countries, except Costa Rica, where education expenditures were first and teachers were valued more than soldiers.

The liberals failed to reach the rural poor, which remained the source of manpower for the material progress that was enjoyed by the select few. Liberal governments ruthlessly suppressed labor organizations. Under such conditions, the image of the rural masses as shiftless and lazy was strengthened.

The banana industry significantly affected Central American development. Bananas first became important in Costa Rica in the mid-1880s. By the end of the nineteenth century, the Tropical Trading and Transport Company developed a large banana trade between Costa Rica and the Gulf Coast of the United States. In 1899 the Tropical Company merged with the Boston Fruit Company, forming the United Fruit Company (UFCO), destined to dominate the region's banana industry.

Expanding into other Central American countries, UFCO developed both the Pacific and Caribbean coasts, building railroads into the interior of each nation. In 1912 it brought control of the region's rail transport under its International Railways of Central America (IRCA). A year later it founded the Tropical Radio and Telegraph Company, which controlled radio communications not only between Central America and the United States, but also throughout Central America. Transportation service was poor, expensive and linked Central America only to the outside world. Intraregional transportation systems were not developed, further contributing to isolation of the five nations among themselves.

UFCO's success encouraged other companies to organize, the most notable being the Standard Fruit and Steamship Company which was founded in 1899 and eventually became UFCO's largest competitor. More aggressive was Samuel Zemurray, founder of the Cuyamel Fruit Company in Honduras. Fierce competition developed in the 1920s, with UFCO buying out Cuyamel for $32 million in 1929, but Zemurray became UFCO's president.

Unlike the coffee industry dominated by small *fincas,* locally owned, the banana industry was comprised of large plantations, mostly owned by foreigners. Still they satisfied the positivist-minded liberals who wanted material progress. The banana industry also contributed to an eventual racial problem. In their desire to develop the eastern coastal regions, the fruit companies imported West Indian black laborers. On the positive side, the banana companies, particularly UFCO, successfully battled many tropical diseases affecting both humans and vegetation.

The banana industry satisfied the liberal objective for material progress, but did so at a loss to national sovereignty and economic independence. United States private interests came to play the dominant role in Central America's economy. By 1938 they far outdistanced Britain and Germany in the amount of commerce with the region and, with over $227 million dollars, were the largest investors. This concentration of wealth contributed to the destruction of Spanish heritage and helped to establish a new oligarchy, which included the foreign capitalists, at the expense of economic and social progress for the masses of people.

These developments, however, significantly contributed to the seeds of change. Economic development accelerated the growth of urban centers, which stimulated both the rise of a middle sector and wide-spread lower class poverty. The middle sector came to include the managers and administrators of the new commercial enterprises, university students and professors, journalists, and professionals.

With relative affluence, they appeared satisfied with their material progress, but not with their inability to participate in the political process,which remained in the hands of the oligarchy. Beginning in the 1920s, the middle sector sought constitutional government, and in the 1930s became targets of the dictators oppressive actions.

Urban development also spawned slums as employers denied workers adequate wages to satisfy basic human needs. Government policies failed to consider this small but potentially important political group of urban poor. In fact, efforts at labor unionization, or demands for improved wages and working conditions, were branded Marxist and ruthlessly suppressed. Communist organizations did appear, first in Guatemala in 1924 and even in Costa Rica by 1930. The Central American Labor Council (COCA) promoted trade union organization and distributed communist propaganda from 1925 to 1930. Pressure for improving the workers' lot also came from the League of Nations and International Labor Organization. The results were laws limiting the work week to 48 hours, provisions for overtime pay and workmen's compensation, and low cost housing. Employers and governments, however, ignored the laws.

The Great Depression and emergence of the dictators in the 1930s retarded labor's growth. Communism was outlawed and suppressed in each country, except Costa Rica. Even here León Cortéz promised, in his successful 1938 presidential campaign, to save the country from the "red hordes of communism."

Economic developments, like those in the political arena, contributed to divergent interests in society. The elite continued to govern at the expense of the middle sector and particularly rural labor. By the late 1930s both of these latter groups were denied participation in the political and social apparatus of the region. The lack of political participation and economic frustration provided the seeds of a potentially volatile situation.

Post World War II

Although the two dominating themes of pre-World War II Central America—the liberal-conservative political struggle and the drive for unity—again emerged after 1945, the most significant factor of this era was the revolution of rising expectations. The liberal-conservative contest was best evidenced by the Costa Rica-Nicaraguan controversies in 1948 and 1955, which pitted the forces of José Figueres against those of Anastasio Somoza. In the political sense, Figueres represented the new trends and Somoza symbolized the remnants of an oligarchy which would be challenged throughout the region by the 1980s.

Regional unity took an economic, rather than political aspect in 1960, with the formation of the Central American Common Market (CACM), essentially a free trade association that anticipated economic integration. Following a brief period of success, CACM floundered after 1966. Its goals were shattered by the 1969 "Soccer War" between Honduras and El Salvador, the oil crisis and subsequent inflation of the 1970s, and the political turmoil late in that decade.

Overriding all was the revolution of rising expectations, a movement by middle and lower socioeconomic groups for a greater role in the political process and improvement in living standards. As noted earlier, the region's economic and political developments after World War I spawned this movement. A new group to Central American politics, the middle sector comprised professionals, white collar management, intellectuals and skilled labor. This group enjoyed relative affluence but was denied political participation by the traditional Liberal and Conservative parties, and by the dictators that dominated the 1930s. The lower socioeconomic groups included unskilled urban labor and rural peasants, who provided the manpower for the agricultural elite. Spokesmen for these underprivileged workers sought improvement in their living standards, but were suppressed by the traditional parties and given lip service by the dictators.

Both groups were greatly affected by World War II. The middle sector was encouraged by the Allied goal to end tyranny, which in Central America was translated to mean an end of the dictatorships. The lower socioeconomic groups, which experienced a degree of prosperity because of the region's contributions to the Allied war effort, now sought to sustain this prosperity. The success of these groups varied from country to country within the region.

Post-1945 Central American politics were characterized by the struggle of the established elite in each country to keep the new forces from participating in the political process. The history of each country in this respect differed until the late 1970s, at which time violence threatened the entire region because, as before, the unsettling influence of the internal political dynamics of one country threatened the stability of its neighbors.

The Democratic Model: Costa Rica

Costa Rica is traditionally identified as a political democracy because there was a peaceful transfer of power at regular four year intervals. The pressure for basic structural change first emerged in the early 1930s with the founding of the Communist Party, which promised to transform completely the Costa Rican economic system so that one group could no longer exploit another. This pledge threatened the coffee growers, but appealed to the lower classes. The party's popularity was measured by the estimated 15,000 votes, of some 90,000 cast, it received in the 1940 presidential election. Although party leader Manuel Mora was the only party member elected to Congress until 1944, party rallies drew crowds as high as large 20,000. Recognition of lower class needs was reflected in several legislative acts, particularly during the presidency of Rafael Calderón Guardia (1940-1944). There were land distribution projects, expansion of the banana industry to provide more employment, and a sweeping Labor Code in 1943. The contrast in living standards between rich and poor remained, however.

The Costa Rican political system was threatened with extinction following the 1944 presidential election, when National Republican (PRN) candidate Teodoro Picado struck a deal with Mora, leader of the Vanguard Party, successor in name only to the Communist Party. In return for promises of political support, Mora gained Picado's assurances to accelerate economic and social reforms. Picado won the election, the most fraudulent in Costa Rican history, but his followers did not win control of the unicameral congress. Mora delivered on his promise of support, but Picado was unable to implement reforms. National politics stagnated for the next four years.

From 1944 to 1948 two new political parties emerged, both in opposition to the leftist leaning PRN and the traditional parties representing the elite. Newspaper editor Otilio Ulate headed the National Union Party (PNU), which represented the middle sector's desire for constitutional government, but took a conservative stand on social issues. The Social Democratic Party, headed by José Figueres, was composed largely of middle class businessmen and students who favored not only constitutional government, but also social welfare programs. Both new parties vehemently opposed the Marxist ideology of Manuel Mora.

Tensions increased as the 1948 election approached, a contest that narrowed to a struggle between Ulate and Calderón. Ulate won the February 8, 1948 election, but the National Electoral Tribunal refused to validate the results, igniting a two month civil war. In April, Figueres directed the opposition forces to victory over government troops which received aid from the Nicaraguan and Honduran dictators, Anastasio Somoza and Tiburcio Carías, respectively. Figueres claimed he fought to implement democracy and to rid the country of communism. In the course of subsequent events, a broader based democracy was established and, although communism was outlawed briefly, the government greatly expanded its economic and social activities.

For eighteen months after the civil war, Figueres directed a *junta*, which wrote a new constitution. When the document was completed in November 1949, Ulate was installed as president. He demonstrated both conservative and reformist tendencies. He did nothing to abolish existing social welfare programs but ignored some, such as the 10% tax on incomes above $10,000, and tempered others, such as permitting private banks to co-exist with national institutions.

Starting with the election of Figueres in 1953 through that of Luis Alberto Monge in 1982, elections have been free expressions of the popular will. Figueres accelerated government-sponsored reforms in public works, health care, education, housing, and social services. Presidents since have continued the process. Agricultural diversification (sugar and grains) along with increased industrialization of nonbasic consumer goods (chemicals and metal works) and an expansion of basic consumer goods (meat, grain processing, and dairy products) have contributed to the nation's economic growth, and offered both urban and rural labor an increased living standard. The middle sector's opportunities have expanded with technocratic positions in government and the private sector. The improved living standards can be measured by job diversification, a high literacy rate, improved housing and fewer infectious diseases by the late 1970s (Tables I through IV).

Neither industrialization nor integration into the Central American Common Market reduced Costa Rica's dependence on foreign commerce; both in fact increased its economic dependence. Coffee, bananas, meat and sugar have remained the major exports, and raw materials and manufactured goods the chief imports. This dependency was revealed during the 1973 and 1977 oil shortages. Since then, according to one labor group, basic food costs have soared by 400% and gasoline by 700%. During 1982 alone, electricity costs increased 137% and water 108%. Inflation has cut the purchasing power of the average Costa Rican by 45% from 1980 to 1983. All of this has contributed to a foreign debt—both public and private—of over $4 billion, or roughly 78% of the current GNP. Economists predicted a

TABLE I
Economically Active Population
(Percentage of Work Force)

	Year	Agriculture Hunting Forestry, Fishing	Mining	Manufact- uring	Con- Services	Electricity Water, Gas and Sanitary Commerce	cations	Transport Storage, Communi- Services
Costa Rica	1973	36.4	0.3	11.9	6.7	0.9	11.6	4.3	22.6
El Salvador	1978	41.0	0.3	14.2	5.4	0.5	15.5	3.8	18.6
Guatemala	1979	57.2	0.1	13.7	4.1	0.3	7.4	2.6	12.5
Honduras	1977	60.9	0.3	12.0	3.3	0.3	8.1	2.8	12.3
Nicaragua	1977	42.0	0.1	16.1	4.8	0.6	13.2	2.9	19.7

Source: James W. Wilke (ed.), **Statistical Abstract for Latin America**, vol. 23, Los Angeles, UCLA-Latin America Center, 1982, p.175.

$200 million shortfall on foreign export earnings and service on the public debt in 1983 alone. President Monge finds himself caught between pressures from international lending agencies for greater austerity and popular demand for increased wages and continued social services. Such uneasiness raises fear that the Costa Rican model of progress may end and that it may be affected by political turmoil similar to that of its neighbors.

Repression of Communists: Guatemala

The dictatorship of Jorge Ubico ended in July 1944 as a result of middle sector pressure. The new forces set in motion a democratic and social reform movement, which lasted until 1954. Thereafter, the military became the final arbiter of Guatemalan politics.

Following Ubico's fall from power, an idealistic university professor Juan José Arévalo was elected president. His vague philosophy of "Spiritual Socialism" was translated into such legislative actions as labor and rent control laws, social security, educational reform and a program of industrialization, all of which sought benefits for the working class at the expense of landowners and business. Arévalo (1944-1950) was unable to fully implement these programs because of upper class resistance and constant plots to overthrow him.

One factor of major importance was the matter of communist influence in the government. With newfound freedom in 1944, some 200 local communists, with no international connection, achieved influential government positions during Arévalo's administration. The communist issue not only frightened the landowning elite, but also split the military, eventually resulting in the assassination of the army's more moderate spokesman Colonel Francisco Javier Arana in 1949. Chief of Staff Jacabo Arbenz Guzmán, more sympathetic to forces demanding accelerated reform, was elected president in 1950, and immediately implemented a reform program that moved the government further left.

Within a year, the government nationalized the U.S.-owned electric company and 234,000 acres of UFCO land on the Pacific. It also threatened to nationalize another 174,000 acres on the Atlantic. Private landowners, who also withheld acreage from cultivation, were threatened with its loss. Arbenz sought to redistribute this land to individual peasants and collective Indian villages. Such action struck directly at the old oligarchy, which found support in exiled military men Carlos Castillo Armas and Miguel Ydígoras Fuentes, and the Church. In April 1954, Archbishop Mariano Rossell y Arellano called for Guatamalans to rise up and rid the country of the

TABLE II
Housing, Households and Facilities

	Year	Average Rooms per Dwelling	Average Persons per Room	Piped Water	Electricity	Toilet
Costa Rica	1973	4.0	1.4	81.0%	68.8%	46.2%
El Salvador	1971	1.7	3.1	26.0%	34.1%	41.3%
Guatemala	1964	2.0	2.6	29.5%	22.0%	30.6%
Honduras	1961	2.3	2.4	24.9%	14.6%	19.8%
Nicaragua	1971	2.2	n.a.	27.9%	40.9%	19.3%

Source: James W. Wilke (ed.), **Statistical Abstract for Latin America**, vol. 17, Los Angeles, UCLA-Latin American Center, 1976, p.112.

TABLE III
Education Profile

	Expenditures			Illiteracy, Age 15 and over (% of total population)			
	Year	% of GNP	% of total Public Expenditure	Year	Total	Urban	Rural
Costa Rica	1976	6.6	30.1	1973	11.6	4.9	17.0
El Salvador	1977	3.7	26.0	1975	37.9	n.a.	n.a.
Guatemala	1976	1.7	13.2	1973	53.9	28.6	68.6
Honduras	1978	n.a.	15.2	1974	43.1	n.a.	n.a.
Nicaragua	1978	n.a.	12.8	1971	42.5	19.5	65.4

Source: James W. Wilkie (ed.), **Statistical Abstract for Latin America**, vol. 23, Los Angeles, UCLA-Latin American Center, 1982, p.143.

"communists," a term used freely by the oligarchy to describe anyone wanting to alter the status quo.

With assistance from the U.S. Central Intelligence Agency (CIA),
Castillo directed an invasion of Guatemala in June 1954. He met little resistance from the army, already threatened with extinction by
an Arbenz plan to create a peasant militia. Castillo replaced Arbenz
and ruled until his assassination in 1957. Castillo repressed communism and effectively subverted all reform laws on the books. UFCO's
land was returned, labor was removed as a major political force, and
the Church regained some of its privileges, particularly the right to
own property. In short, the old liberal oligarchy regained its pre-1944
position and, protected by the military, has retained that position to
the present. Ydígoras succeeded Castillo, and remained in office until
1963, when Colonel Enrique Peralta Azurdia replaced him. Julio
César Mendez Montenegro, a member of the coffee growing elite
was elected in 1966. Guatemala's only civilian president since 1950,
Montenegro presided but did not rule. The army remained the final
authority. It returned to the forefront with the fraudulent presidential elections of Colonel Carlos Arana in 1977, General Kjell
Langerud García in 1974, General Fernando Romero Lucas García
in 1978, and General Angel Anibal Guevara in 1982.

An unsuccessful revolt in November 1960 proved a turning point
in Guatemala's post World War II history. Survivors of the revolt,
led by Marcos Aurelio Yon Sosa, formed the Thirteenth of November Revolutionary Movement (MR-13), a new Marxist group that
lasted for a decade. A second guerilla group, the Rebel Armed
Forces (FAC), was founded by Luis A. Turcio Lima and collabor-
ated with the outlawed, underground Communist Party. With support from university students and leftist army elements, these
guerilla groups contributed to a great sense of insecurity in the
1960s. In response, right wing terrorist groups—The White Hand
and an Eye for an Eye—appeared. President Peralta, with United
States assistance, checked, but did not suppress the insurgents, thus
providing a facade of stability.

Beginning with Colonel Arana in 1970, the government launched
a systematic terror campaign. According to the Committee of Relatives of Disappeared Persons, some 15,000 Guatemalans disappeared during his administration. General Langerud softened the
government stand during 1975 and 1976, permitting unions, student
groups, professional societies, *campesino* organizations, and moderate political parties to appear, and public demonstrations to take
place. Fearful of their potential political importance, however,
Langerud initiated a program of selective assassination, beginning

with the killing of labor leader Mario López Larave in June 1977. Public protest led to further repression, which brought condemnation from human rights groups and subsequent suspension of United States military aid. The repression continued under Lucas García. Beginning in 1978 death squad killings were directed against town mayors, teachers, health care workers, and labor and corporate leaders. In 1981, Amnesty International declared that anyone who opposed the government, or was thought to oppose the government, was systematically seized, tortured and murdered. The brief hope that the 1982 presidential election might bring a reprieve ended with the killing of civilian political leaders Manuel Colom Argueta and Alberto Fuentes Mohr.

Army Chief of Staff General Efraín Ríos Montt engineered a coup that prevented Anibal Guevara from taking office and immediately ordered an end to urban violence. While this action drew global praise, Montt planned a new rural offensive against the guerillas. He implemented a counter-insurgency movement, as well as a civic action program aimed at winning the peasants over with gifts of food and clothing. But violence dominated. In October 1982, Amnesty International charged that some 2600 people had been massacred, and Mexico accused Guatemala of sending troops across their common border to attack refugees fleeing from the violence.

Montt also initiated a land redistribution program, described as "homesteading," which infuriated the upper class, as did his proposed tax reform program. Middle sector elements became disenchanted with Montt's failure to move quickly toward constitutional government. These factors isolated Montt, caused opposition from key elements of society, and triggered a coup in August 1983 directed by General Oscar Humberto Mejía Victores, a rightist supported by the landowners. The old oligarchial alliance again surfaced to control government.

In an effort to establish credibility in the international community, Mejía Victores decreed elections for a constituent assembly to be held July 1, 1984. Twenty three parties entered candidates, but only two coalitions were of primary importance. The moderate coalition, comprised of the Christian Democrartic Party and Union of the National Center, received 17.2% and 14.5% of the popular vote respectively. The rightest coalition, comprised of the National Liberation Movement and the Nationalistic Authentic Central, received 13.2% of the popular vote. Under complex apportionment guidelines, however, the Supreme Electoral Tribunal awarded the rightest coalition twenty three seats in the constituent assembly and twenty one each to the Christian Democrats and Union of the

National Center. The remaining twenty three seats were divided among the smaller parties. The assembly began its work in September, warned by Mejía Victores not to go beyond its assigned task of writing a new constitution and electoral and civil rights laws. Presidential elections are scheduled for June 1985.

Guatemala's economic development, based on agriculture, has paralleled that of her neighbors. Coffee, cotton, bananas, and sugar provide the largest share of the nation's revenue, in a country where approximately one fourth the arable land is under crop cultivation and where 57% of the labor force is tied to agriculture.

Government tax policies, introduced in the 1960s, sought to encourage private investment. For example, new industries were exempt from import duties for ten years, 100% of their income taxes for five years, and 50% for the next five. Tax benefits also favored expansion of existing industries. Construction was encouraged by exempting new buildings from taxes for several years. Throughout the 1970s, there was constant expansion in the manufacturing and construction industries. But like agriculture, manufacturing has been export-oriented with emphasis on food stuffs, textiles, and wood and metal products. Outside the money economy has been a sizeable Indian group that barters in local markets only.

In 1978, the Guatemalan economy weakened and by 1981 it was in a serious recession. Inflation increased at 11% annually, and the GDP rose only 1% in 1981. Unemployment and underemployment was estimated at 34%. Such adversity contributed to an estimated $1 billion flight of capital by 1981, and a $353 million reduction of international reserves to $30 million.

The nation's industrial development accounted for the increased pressure for political reform by middle sector and urban labor groups. But as the economic situation worsened in the late 1970s, rural opposition groups began to reappear, one result being the shift in emphasis to counter-insurgency by the Montt regime. By late 1981, guerilla groups were active in 21 of Guatemala's 22 provinces. The two largest, both drawing their strength from the rural Indians, were the Marxist-orientated Guerilla Army of the Poor (EGP) and the Revolutionary Organization of the People in Arms (URPA). A third force, the Rebel Armed Forces (FAR), traces its origins to the communist movement of the late 1960s. These groups attacked army outposts and barracks and distributed propaganda to rural villagers. They united in January 1982 under the title Guatemalan National Revolutionary Unity (URNG). Its program called for an end to Indian repression, elimination of the native and foreign capitalist elite, and total political freedom and participation in government.

A month later 26 *campesino*, labor, and middle sector groups, along with religious leaders and exiles from the 1944-1954 period, formed the Guatemalan Patriotic Unitary Committee (CGUP). Subsequently, the two leading opposition parties—the United Front of the Revolution (FUR) and Social Democrats (PSD)—endorsed the CGUP statement that a popular revolutionary war was the only route left to the people. In August 1983, the U.S. State Department estimated that 2500 guerilla forces operated within Guatemala. The Mejía Victores regime and the Guatemalan oligarchy continued to be threatened by substantial opposition from the middle sector as well as urban and rural labor. The Church, under new Archbishop Prospero Penades Barrio, took a more distant stance from the military in July 1984. The archbishop asserted that the guerilla movement was not crushed; that the guerillas were only in tactical retreat. Violence abated, but atrocities continued. Through October 1984, an estimated fifty bodies per week were found on roadsides and in the underbrush. Guatemala remained a tinderbox.

The Military Rules: Honduras

Honduras is the poorest of the five Central American states with an annual per capita income of $280, causing one United States diplomat to observe that there is no great disparity of wealth, because even the rich are poor. Like its neighbors, Honduras has an agriculturally based economy. Bananas remain the chief export, but under the control of foreign companies—United Brands (successor to UFCO) and Standard Fruit Company. Estimates indicate that Honduras receives only 12 cents of every dollar of banana export revenues.However, there is no local oligarchy similar to Costa Rica's coffee barons or Guatemala's cotton planters.

Postwar politics in Honduras have not paralleled the experiences of its neighbors. In 1944, middle sector pressure in the form of a few demonstrations and petitions failed to unseat dictator Tiburcio Carías. He remained in office until 1948, when he stepped aside in favor of his hand-picked successor, Juan Manuel Gálvez, who governed until 1954. Three years of military interference in government ended with a new constitution and the election of Ramón Villeda Morales in 1957. Frequent uprisings, conflicts with foreign-owned companies and border disputes with Nicaragua marred Villeda Morales's six-year administration. In 1959, he created a 2500 man Civil Guard, independent of the army, and loyal to the president. For reasons still unclear he disarmed the Guard shortly before the October 1963 elections, an action that directly led to a coup. Air

Force Colonel Osvaldo López was installed as president, beginning eighteen years of military rule.

Transition toward civilian government began with the April 1980 election of a constituent assembly. The centrist Liberal Party captured 35 seats and the conservative National Party 33. When Liberal Party candidate Roberto Suazo Córdoba won the November 1981 presidential elections, many observers claimed that Honduras had become a democratic state. On the other hand, critics maintained that armed forces Commander Brigadier General Gustavo Alvarez Martínez was the real power in the country. He ruled the military with a heavy hand and limited the opportunities for officers to advance in rank. Internal discontent within the military resulted in a barrack's coup on March 31, 1984. Alvarez Martínez was replaced by Air Force General Walter Lopez. The change, however, did not signal a change in Honduran foreign policy, nor in the military's role in government.

President Suazo Códoba's nationalistic economic policies caused discontent among the Honduran business community. During the first weekend in November 1984, the United States FBI arrested seven former Honduran businessmen living in Miami, Florida on charges of plotting to oust Sauzo Códoba. Also implicated was General José Bueso Rosa, military attaché to the Honduran embassy in Santiago, Chile. Arrests followed in Tegucigalpa and President Sauzo Códoba outlawed, by decree, the Association of Progress for Honduras, a civic organization of conservative businessmen, labor and peasant leaders founded by former armed forces chief General Alvarez Martínez.

Most Honduran workers are tied to the agricultural sector, working for large landowners. A land distribution program, dating from the 1960s, remains dormant. During that decade Honduras experienced an annual growth rate of 5.3%, which declined following the 1969 "Soccer War" with El Salvador and the 1974-1975 oil shock. Recovery came in 1976, lasting until 1980 when Honduras got caught up in the region's political turmoil. Growth in exports and increased private investment provided funds for an ambitious infrastructure program—roads, port facilities and hydroelectric power. However, the recent Central American crisis contributed to an economic slowdown in 1981 and caused an estimated $500 million flight of capital, a $300 million federal budget deficit and a 24% unemployment rate.

While not plagued with the political turmoil of its neighbors, Honduras has economic and social conditions that cause unrest. Inadequate housing, poor medical attention, and a high illiteracy rate (Tables

I through IV) indicate the severity of Honduran poverty. The business community became restive with the government's increased activity in the nation's economic affairs, and the increasing presence of the military causes doubts about the extent of civilian government.

TABLE IV

Principle Causes of Death

Costa Rica (1978)	Number	Rate PHTI*	Percentage
All Causes	8,625	405.8	100.0
Malignant Neoplasms	1,447	68.1	16.8
Heart Disease	1,317	61.9	15.3
Accidents	952	44.8	11.0
Cerebrovascular Disease	571	26.9	6.6
Perinatal Mortality	567	26.6	6.6
El Salvador (1974)			
All Causes	20,553	784.9	100.0
Enterites and Other Diahrreal Disease	4,072	104.7	13.3
Accidents	1,835	47.2	6.0
Perinatal Mortality	1,366	35.1	4.5
Homicide, Legal Intervention and War	1,283	33.0	4.2
Influenza and Pneumonia	1,257	32.3	4.1
Bronchitis, Emphysema, Asthma	1,089	28.0	3.6
Heart Disease	1,008	25.9	3.3
Guatemala (1978)			
All Causes	63,998	966.6	100.0
Enteritas and Other Diahrreal Diseases	11,343	171.3	17.7
Influenza, Pneumonia	9,199	139.0	14.4
Perinatal Mortality	5,993	90.5	9.4
Accidents	4,525	68.3	7.1
Heart Diseases	2,397	36.2	3.7
Avitaminoses and Other Nutritional Deficiencies	2,173	32.8	3.4
Measles	2,027	30.6	3.2

Honduras (1976)	Number	Rate PHTI*	Percentage
All Causes	18,168	567.8	100.0
Enteritis and Other			
Diahrreal Diseases	2,212	69.1	12.2
Heart Diseases	1,474	46.1	8.1
Homicide, Legal			
Intervention	1,145	35.8	6.3
Influenza, Pneumonia	808	25.3	4.4
Bronchitis, Emphysema,			
Asthma	605	18.9	3.3
Malignant Neoplasms	431	13.5	2.4
Nicaragua (1978)			
All Causes	9,208	382.1	100.0
Heart Diseases	1,368	56.7	14.9
Enteritis and Other			
Diahrreal Diseases	898	37.3	9.8
Accidents	718	29.8	7.8
Malignant Neoplasms	309	12.8	3.4
Homicide, Legal			
Intervention and War	302	12.5	3.3
Influenza, Pneumonia	288	11.9	3.1

*PHTI means Per Hundred Thousand Inhabitants

Source: James W. Wilkie (ed.), **Statistical Abstract for Latin America**, Vol.23, Los Angeles, UCLA-Latin American Center, 1982, pp. 112-114.

A Dynasty Crumbles: Nicaragua

Middle sector pressure and a split in the Liberal Party forced Anastasio Somoza to withdraw a proposed constitutional amendment in 1944 that would have permitted his reelection in 1947. Somoza's influence remained sufficient so that Liberals nominated 72 year old Leonardo Argüello, who won the 1947 elections, which were controlled by the National Guard. When Argüello attempted to act independently, Somoza engineered a coup and forced the acceptance of his own uncle Victor Ramón y Reyes as president. Somoza returned to power via the ballot box in 1950, and ruled until his assassination in September 1956. Power passed to his two sons Luis and Anastasio Somoza DeBayle, Luis as president and Anastasio as commander of the National Guard.

Although Luis Somoza kept his promise not to seek reelection in 1963, nor permit any relative to be a candidate, the Somoza brothers imposed the candidacy of René Shick upon the Liberal Party. He easily captured the presidency because Conservative Party candidate Fernando Agüero boycotted the contest when the Somozas refused supervision of the election by the Organization of American States (OAS). With opposition leaders jailed on election day, Anatasio Somoza captured the 1967 presidential contest. Mounting opposition forced him to postpone the scheduled 1971 elections until 1974, and install an interim junta in May 1972, a move that did not conceal Somoza as the real authority.

The Somoza family controlled not only Nicaraguan politics, but also the country's economy, amassing a fortune estimated in 1979 to be from $60 to $300 million. To this end the family employed several methods. The government granted concessions, for a high price, to both local and foreign capitalists to exploit rubber, gold, and timber. Bribes were extracted from illegal gambling, prostitution, and clandestine alcoholic beverage operations. Laws were passed to restrict certain imports, usually those pursued by Somoza's political opponents. Then contraband operations were established to circumvent the laws and sell the merchandise in Somoza family operated-stores. The senior Somoza conducted an illegal cattle export trade to Costa Rica and Panama and, for a fee, permitted others to do the same. Anti-German legislation during World War II resulted in Somoza's seizure of 56 cattle ranches and 46 coffee plantations. National Bank loans, not available to others, permitted the Somozas to build and control railroad interests, lake ferries, a sugar refinery, milk pasturizing plants, the country's only cement plant, several electric power plants, textile mills, ship and air lines, and the newspaper *Novedades.*

Between 1945 and 1972, the enormous concentration of wealth and political power in the Somoza family contributed to the formation of several indentifiable opposition groups and to an atmosphere characterized by threats and violence. The Somozas responded with repression. Brutality and loss of civil rights increased with each episode. Upper class opposition included the traditional Conservative Party, whose leadership came from several families traced to the nineteenth century—Chamorro, Caudra, Zavala, Solórzano and Pasos. After 1950, the groups' most visible spokesman was Pedro Joaquín Chamorro, editor of the opposition newspaper *La Prensa.* After 1950, younger conservatives, disillusioned with their elders co-opting by Somoza, formed the Popular Christian Democratic Movement (MPDC). Taking control of the Conservative Party, the MPDC was responsible for Agüro's nomination in 1963 and 1967, but deserted the party to join other less conservative groups when Agüro agreed to the 1972 junta. A second upper class group were the Dissident Liberals, which originated at the start of the 1944 crisis, but by 1970 it remained only a small conclave. Like the Conservatives, their roots were traced to the nineteenth century. Both factions represented the historic struggle of "outs" wanting "in" and not any desire for real democratic government.

Middle sector groups rallied around the Independent Liberal Party (PLI), which also evolved from the 1944 crisis. While it supported opposition candidates to the Somozas, the PLI was more effective in organizing political groups. The most significant of these groups was the Democratic Youth Front (FYD), organized in 1946 to mobilize high school and university students. Over the years its leaders, including a Sandinista founder Tomás Borge Martínez, were imprisoned, exiled, tortured or put to death. A second middle sector group, the Nicaraguan Social Christian Party (PSCN) organized in 1948, did not become significant until after 1963 when it collected MPDC members who had deserted the Conservative Party. The PSCN won two congressional seats in the 1967 elections and, at the beginning of the 1970s many observers believed it offered the best hope for the future. There were several middle sector unions in the cities. Among the most notable were the National Association of Educators (ANDEN), the Federation of Nicaraguan Teachers (FMN), the National Employees Union (UNE) and Association of Women Confronting National Problems (AMPRONAC). Only after 1972, however, were these groups able to successfully press their demands against the government.

Prior to 1972, the Nicaraguan peasants were never adequately represented. The Socialist Party (PSN) and the virtually non-existent Communist Party were outlawed in 1950; thereafter they operated underground. The Socialists made little effort to appeal to the peasants, whom they considered retrograde and lacking in revolutionary potential. The peasants, manipulated by landowners, held blind allegiances to the traditional Liberal and Conservative parties. Their conditions worsened after 1972 and lacking land, education, housing, and health care (Tables I through IV), they became a potentially important political force.

That potential was realized by the Sandinista National Liberation Front (FSLN)—a movement that originated with the 1944-48 and 1959-61 student protest. Its prime leader was Carlos Fonseca Amador, whose exile travels took him to Mexico, the Soviet Union, and Cuba. He believed that the only way to bring down the Somozas was through a guerilla revolution, similar to Fidel Castro's in Cuba.

With old friends Silvio Mayorga and Tomás Borge Martínez he founded the FSLN in 1961. Between 1961 and 1967, their small band robbed a few banks to satisfy their financial needs and carried out a few raids, only to be defeated by the National Guard. After 1967, the leadership developed new principles and strategies to build a rural base. In the meantime, continued bank robberies and periodic terrorism kept them in the public eye. By 1970, the FSLN had become a well-organized insurgent force, with a support among peasants in rural areas and students in the urban centers. Still, as the decade began, the extent of FSLN support was not known.

The varied sources of opposition to the Somoza dynasty still were not able to crystallize on their own. The unexpected catalyst to Somoza's downfall was a devastating earthquake in December 1972, which destroyed half of Managua and killed an estimated 10,000 people. In the quake's immediate aftermath, National Guardsmen, more concerned with the well-being of their families, were not available to maintain order and safety in Managua. Also, Anastasio Somoza brushed aside the ruling junta and took personal control of governmental decision-making. In the relief and reconstruction efforts that followed the quake, Somoza supporters were given first priority at the expense of the poor, and charges of corruption were widespread. Although undocumented, Nicaraguans generally believed that Somoza personally profited from the disaster. Finally Somoza used the disaster to solidify his own position as the 1974 Liberal Party presidential candidate. Unable to reach an agreement with his political opposition, Somoza directed the enactment of laws providing for control of the press, making it a crime to defame the government and a crime not to vote.

These actions caused the opposition groups to coalesce. First, the Democratic Liberation Union (UDEL) brought together several upper and middle class groups, which sought reform through the system rather than by revolution. More dramatic was the seizure of José María Castillo's home on December 27, 1974, by an FSLN detachment. A Somoza supporter and former Agricultural Minister, Castillo was hosting a party that included several government officials. Archbishop Obando y Bravo mediated the crisis, which provided the FSLN with a $1 million ransom, release of political prisoners, and government publication and radio broadcast of FSLN communiques.

Subsequently Somoza declared a state of seige and permitted the Guard to brutally attack northern rural villages suspected of being strongholds of the FSLN. These actions were condemned by both the Catholic Church and Amnesty International. Somoza recognized his growing isolation by lifting the state of seige in September 1977 and accepting Archbishop Obando y Bravo's call for a dialogue between the regime and moderate forces.

The assassination of *La Prensa* editor Pedro Joaquín Chamorro on January 10, 1978, caused the upper and middle sector groups to join forces. First, the UDEL successfully closed down about 80% of the nation's businesses with a general strike January 24th. By July 1978, the Broad Opposition Front (FAO) was organized, bringing together the UDEL, the Committee of Twelve (FSLN's cabinet), the Nicaraguan Democratic Movement (a broad based business and professional group), and the Conservative and Christian Democratic parties. Uprisings in Masaya, León, and Diriamba, and strikes by teachers and industrial transport and hospital workers, further measured the extent of opposition to Somoza.

In August 1978, the Tercerista faction of the FSLN, led by Edén Pastora and Humberto Ortega, seized the National Palace taking several prisoners. As before, a ransom was paid, political prisoners released, and FSLN declarations calling for Somoza's ouster published by the government. This act precipitated another general strike, called for by the FAO, and coordinated with FSLN assaults against National Guard stations in several cities. In suppressing the concomitant uprisings in Matagalpa and Jinotepe, the Guard bombed, strafed, and shelled civilian housing, summarily executed prisoners, raped women, and pillaged homes. In light of this extensive unrest and violence, the OAS unsuccessfully sought to mediate the crisis.

After a few months of relative calm FSLN forces again struck at major cities in April and May 1979. Again they were driven out by a ferocious National Guard response, but at a great loss of men and materiél to the Guard. What proved to be the final offensive began with a general strike on June 4, 1979, and culminated in Somoza's fleeing the country July 17. The broad-based opposition denied Somoza any support other than the National Guard, which itself dwindled in the face of continued losses to the coordinated FSLN final military offensive.

On July 19, FSLN forces took control of the country. Its five-man provisional government, formed a month earlier, included only one FSLN leader, Daniel Ortega. Two others, Moisés Hassan Morales and Sergio Ramírez, were closely allied to the Sandinistas. The two others were considered moderates, wealthy industrialist Alfonso Robelo and the wife of slain *La Prensa* editor, Violeta Barrios de Chamorro. The junta inherited an economy in ruins and a government ravaged by civil war. Somoza left a national debt of $1.6 million with only $3.5 million in international reserves. The Gross Domestic Product (GDP) declined 25% in 1979. Most government officials and midlevel bureaucrats had fled the country.

The revolutionary government announced its intention to create a "New Nicaragua," meaning a reconstructed national economy and a society with reduced class inequality and an improved standard of living, increased economic opportunity for the lower classes, and the establishment of a democracy. The last goal, democracy, became the first one to affect the Sandinista's image at home and abroad. Rather than a liberal, representative constitutionalism, the Sandinistas intended a more corporatistic type of government, with elections postponed until the establishment of national institutions capable of defending the revolution. In addition, the promise of economic pluralism appeared jeopardized by increased government participation in the economy. The Inter-American Development Bank reported that from 1979 to 1980 the Nicaraguan government increased its share of the GDP by 37%. These tendencies contributed to the resignation from the junta of Violeta Chamorro and Alfonso Robelo, leaving only Marxist-oriented members. Press censorship, increased income taxes, and postponement of elections until 1985 caused middle and upper sector Nicaraguans to leave the country with as much of their wealth as possible.

In Honduras these groups formed a counterrevolutionary force, known as the *contras* to topple the Sandinistas. Edén Pastora, an FSLN war hero, left in July 1981 for Costa Rica to organize his own movement against the regime. Both groups charged the Sandinistas were communists, but failed to cooperate in their efforts because Pastora saw the *contras* as *Somocistas*, intent only on returning to power. Over the next three years, the Sandinistas increased their restrictive measures, resulting in charges of human rights violations by several international groups, became embroiled with the Church, expanded the government role in the economy, and increased the presence of Cubans, Russians and East Europeans. By 1984 these developments caused the Sandinistas to become the major focus of President Ronald Reagan's Central American policy.

Under economic duress, political pressure, and social unrest, the Sandinistas announced in January 1984 that elections for a president, vice president and constituent assembly would be held in November 1984, a year ahead of schedule. The objective was to win a measure of legitimacy, which in turn would bring in badly needed foreign economic assistance and perhaps pressure the Reagan administration to halt its funding of the *contras*.

Legitimate opposition was not forthcoming. The Democratic Coordinating Committee, representing the Liberal Constitutional, Social Christian and Social Democratic parties, two labor federations and several business groups, withdrew from the elections in August. Its would be presidential candidate, Arturo Cruz, demanded that a consituent assembly be elected first. This would have provided the moderates an opportunity to make their political case against the Sandinistas. In October Liberal Independent Party candidate Virgilio Godoy also withdrew, asserting that the elections were meaningless.

Six parties remained, but Sandinista candidate Daniel Ortega was the odds on favorite because the other parties had little popular support. Given the political weakness of the opposition, the election was little more than a referendum on Sandinista policies. It remains to be seen whether the Sandinistas overwhelming victory on November 4 will gain them the international support that they seek.

The Sandinistas, despite their political victory, were still faced with a severe economic crisis. Shortages of essentials, from beans to toilet paper, remained. A black market continued to flourish. Inflation was rampant. The Church remained confrontational. The poor protested the unpopular military draft and failure to satisfy wage demands. Large cotton and coffee producers held back production in face of threatening government policies, and fear of expropriation. These factors contributed to the government's inability to meet international financial obligations and resulted in the World Bank's suspension of loans to Nicaragua.

Opposition forces representing all elements of Nicaraguan society—upper, middle and lower sectors—brought down the Somoza dynasty. Beginning in 1980, Sandinista policies contributed to the departure of numerous upper and middle class families. Restrictions placed on those who remained behind, plus the emphasis given to the lower socio-economic sector, caused many observers to compare the Nicaraguan experience with Castro's revolution in Cuba.

The Oligarchy Under Attack: El Salvador

The first Central American dictator to be ousted by middle sector pressure in 1944 was Maximiliano Hernández Martínez of El Salvador. Student protests over his efforts to gain, illegally, a fourth presidential term set in motion a chain of events that resulted in a nationwide general strike in May and led to Hernández's resignation.

The junta that followed, led by National Defense Minister Andrés Menéndez, represented the middle sector. Among the plethora of political parties formed after Hernández's overthrow was the Democratic Union headed by physician Arturo Romero. The party's economic and social program was an anathema to the coffee growers, but represented the views of the middle and lower sectors. Romero's growing popularity contributed to a military coup on October 21, 1944, led by Colonel Osmin Aguirre y Salinas, who convinced the coffee growers that his group was a reasonable alternative to the "radical" Romero group. In anticipation of government control, the opposition withdrew from participation in the January 1945 presidential elections, won by General Castenada Castro. In less than a year, Salvador had come full circle. The promise of democracy failed and dictatorship returned.

Castenada pushed many liberal reform programs through congress—minimum wages, regulation of working hours, social security and housing. None was implemented during his four year term, however, because of conservative opposition, best demonstrated by approximately 20 attempts to remove him from office. When Castenada attempted to extend his stay in office, a coup on December 13, 1948, established an interim junta, which governed until elections confirmed Major Oscar Osorio as president in March 1950. Osorio drew his support from the younger military officers and the middle sector. His Revolutionary Party of Democratic Unification (PRUD) became El Salvador's major political party until 1960. Osorio's hand picked successor Lt. Colonel José María Lemus was unopposed in the 1956 presidential contest.

Opposition and violence increased toward the conclusion of Lemus' term, resulting in the coups of October 1960 and January 1961. Lt. Colonel Julio Adalberto Rivera, leader of the second junta, was unopposed in the 1962 presidential election and his chosen successor General Fidel Sánchez was elected president in 1967. The traditional military-landowner oligarchy continued to dominate Salvadoran politics for twenty five years following the overthrow of Hernández.

Although Osorio and Lemus initiated "restrained" social legislation—an extensive housing program, legalization of labor unions, social security, completion of the Lempa River hydroelectric plant, and improved port facilities at Acajutla—there was no improvement in living standards for the Salvadoran masses. If anything, their economic policies of the 1960s, widened the gap between rich and poor and contributed to growing unrest within the middle sector.

Tax laws designed to encourage capital accumulation and industrialization provided the coffee growers, already benefiting from high coffee prices, an opportunity to invest in new areas, along with foreign (largely U.S.) capital. At first industrialization centered around import substitution—the production of goods previously imported. New technology made these industries capital, not labor, intensive. The same was true for foreign investors such as Texas Instruments and Maidenform. The "boom economy" of the 1960s, spurred by industrialization and the Central American Common Market, provided little opportunity for the urban labor sector, where unemployment ranged from 30% to 50%. Rural workers suffered a similar fate. Landowners used improved technology and fertilizers to increase the yields per acre, even in the cotton and sugar fields, which contributed to worker displacement as more land became idle. The number of landless *campesinos* increased from 112,108 in 1961 to 166,922 by 1975. The situation was exacerbated by the 1969 "Soccer War" with Honduras, which further weakened CACM. The Honduran market alone was worth $23 million annually to Salvador.

In the 1970s the oligarchy, particularly in cooperation with U.S. investors, expanded its dominance over the economy. By the decade's end, the oligarchy operated 86% of the agricultural businesses, 55% of the construction and 72% of the manufacturing industries, 53% of the commerce interests and 72% of the service industries. Overall, the Salvadoran oligarchy controlled 66% of the total number of businesses in the country. United States interests accounted for 56% of the total foreign investment in the country and was concentrated in such capital intensive areas as textiles, pharmacuticals, chemicals, petroleum and paper products. Such concentration of wealth contributed a wide disparity of living standards between rich and poor (Tables I through IV).

Political opposition to the oligarchy's control of the government and economy continued to come from the middle sector. Most significant was the Christian Democratic Party (PDC), which was founded in 1961. The party also drew support from the urban workers and poorer classes, the extent of which was unknown because leftist parties were illegal. José Napoleon Duarte became the party's leading spokesman. A second group, the Revolutionary National Movement (MNR), affiliated with the Socialist International, appeared during the 1960s. Like its leader, Guillermo Manuel Ungo, the party intellectualized and therefore did not register significant political growth among its followers, mostly workers in the large industrial enterprises. A third party was the National Democratic Union (UDC), a splinter group of the official PCN, and consisted mostly of younger army officers. The PDC, MNR, and UDC formed the National Opposition Union (UNO) to nominate Duarte for the presidency in 1972. There is much evidence to support Duarte's claim to victory, but the military ensured the installation of PCN candidate Colonel Arturo Armando Molina. With Duarte exiled in Venezuela, the UNO nominated Ernesto Claramount to run against Carlos Humberto Romero in 1977. Romero won amidst obvious signs of corruption and voter intimidation and Claramount was exiled to Costa Rica.

While the middle sector sought to correct national problems through political reform, new groups began to seek redress of grievances through other means. From this perspective, the 1972 election changed the character and direction of Salvadoran politics.

The Catholic Church was the first to speak and act on behalf of the poor. In 1968, at Medellín, Colombia, the Second Episcopal Conference (CELAM II) of Bishops called upon the Church to defend the rights of the oppressed and to establish grassroots organizations to offer a "preferential option for the poor." This action paved the way for liberation theology.

In El Salvador, Church activity began during pastoral week in July 1970 when the three archbishops took issue with existing Salvadoran economic and social structures. Over the next several years, the Church established several hundred Christian Based Communities (CEBs) and trained an estimated 15,000 lay leaders to reach the poor. Among other things the laymen were to preach that the poor had a right to organize to correct their poverty. With Jesuit leadership, the University of Central America was established in San Salvador. It too was committed to reform. In May 1977, Msgr. Oscar Romero was named Archbishop of El Salvador and became a leading spokesman for reform. All of these activities elicited a harsh response from the military and landowners. Repressive measures against the clerics, including torture and death, failed to silence the church spokesmen. The crisis reached a new height in December 1980 with the killing of three American nuns and a lay missionary, and the subsequent assassination of Romero during mass.

The same period saw the emergence of several popular front organizations with Marxist leanings, including the United Popular Action Front (FAPU), the Popular Revolutionary Bloc (BRP), and the 28th of February Popular League (LP-28). Together these groups reached the urban and rural poor. Also two umbrella groups formed, the largest and most important being the Farabundo Marti Front for the National Liberation (FMLN) which brought together five guerrilla organizations of unknown strength. This organization has remained committed to the violent overthrow of the government. The second umbrella group, the Democratic Revolutionary Front (FDR), is the political partner of the FMLN, bringing together organizations that served as support groups for the guerrillas.

Confrontation resulted in violence. The government utilized the Nationalist Democratic Organization (ORDEN), which by 1977 included army reservists and retired security officers. The guerilla groups increased their attacks on the oligarchy and government. By mid-1979 the country was in chaos and on the brink of civil war. Influenced by this and the fall of Somoza in July 1979, a group of young army officers—Colonels Jaime Abdul Gutiérrez, Adolfo Arnoldo Majano, José Guillermo Garcia and Eugenio Vides Casanova—engineered a coup on October 15, 1979. After infighting and adjustments, a new junta was formed in January 1980, under Majano's leadership and included José Napoleon Duarte, the Christian Democratic leader who returned from exile.

The new civilian-military junta initiated a land reform program in March and April 1980 designed to make the rural peasant self-sufficient. This direct attack upon the oligarchy elicited its fierce response. Former National Guard officer Roberto D'Aubuisson denounced the coalition junta as communist and is believed to have been the driving force behind the ensuing right-wing violence. Terror tactics and brutal killings frightened peasants away from the land reform program. The guerillas initially only denounced the program as a hoax, eventually, however, they too attacked the peasants, because they feared the program might be successful. In late 1983 one analyist argued that the landowners would permit the country to fall to the guerrillas rather than permit the land reform program to succeed.

Politically, the reform program was further jeopardized by the results of the March 28, 1982, constituent assembly elections, which placed the Christian Democrats against an array of opposition, including the Nationalist Republican Alliance (ARENA), the Party of National Conciliation (PCN) and the Democratic Action Party (AD). These parties represented the oligarchy. The FMLN refused to participate, claiming that exposure would be suicidal. While the Christian Democrats won 35% of the popular vote and 24 assembly seats, the three rightest parties together collected 65% of the popular vote and 35 assembly seats. No single presidential candidate won a majority of the popular votes forcing a run-off election May 6, 1984, between the top two contenders Christian Democrat José Napoleon Duarte and ARENA leader Roberto D'Aubuisson. Duarte won the run-off election with nearly 54% of the popular vote, and installed as president on June 1, 1984.

Duarte immediately set out to gain international support for his government. In an effort to placate opposition groups in the United States, Duarte promised to personally take charge of the investigation into the murder of two U.S. citizens, killed while working for the A.I.D. in El Salvador. Duarte also traveled to Europe in search of badly needed economic support. Most dramatic was his call for a meeting with rebel leaders; a call issued during an address to the United Nations in October, 1984.

The FDR-FMLN accepted, but claimed that they initiated the process that previous May. The reasons for their acceptance were speculative. The rebel groups appeared split on the issue, with the most militant group, the People's Revolutionary Army (PAR) opposed to any dialogue with the government. The rebel military forces also appeared to be in retreat on the battlefield because of short supplies and in face of the better prepared and equipped government troops. Although a euphoria of popular optimism preceeded the talks, Duarte did not enjoy clear cut support. The military registered its opposition; Roberto D'Aubuisson denounced the meeting as a "circus," and one death squad, The Secret Anticommunist Army, threathened to assassinate the president.

Representatives of both sides met October 15 at La Palma, a rural village in guerrilla-held territory, some sixty miles from San Salvador. Included in Duarte's entourage was Defense Minister General Eugenio Vides Casanova. The FDR-FMLN representatives included Guillermo Manuel Ungo and Rubén Zamora. Notably absent was Jaoquí Villalobos, leader of the militant PAR faction. The four and one half hour meeting, presided over by Archbishop Arturo Rivera y Damas, produced no startling results, only an agreement to establish a twelve-man commission. Duarte refused to accede to the rebel demands for immediate government power-sharing and integration of its forces into the government's military establishment. The rebels refused Duarte's suggestion that they immediately lay down their arms, accept amnesty, and participate in the nations's political process.

Salvador's civil war remained at impasse. the struggle between the oligarchy and land reformers continued. Democracy remained a goal of the middle sector, and improved living standards only a dream to the poor.

Summary

In its political and economic development, Central America passed through three distinct phases before reaching its contemporary crisis. During each of these phases—colonial period, the Liberal-Conservative struggle, and the dictators of the 1930s—the seeds of the contemporary crisis were reenforced. The economic, social, and political disparities among the various components of society were clearly established by the end of World War II, after which the challenge to the existing order came forward. Reflecting differences of the past, each of the five countries has been affected differently, but certain common characteristics prevail. Most important is the fact that the region's historical experience laid the groundwork for the contemporary crisis.

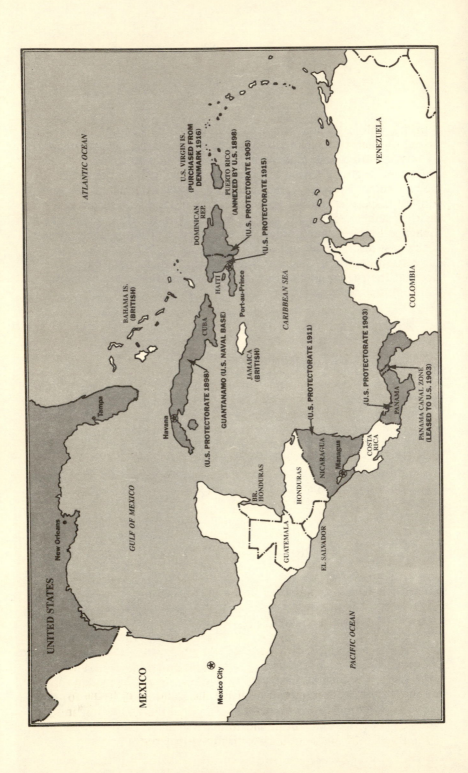

II

United States—Central American Relations

The most consistent feature of United States policy toward Central America has been the effort to keep Europeans out. During the first half of the nineteenth century, it was largely British interests that were to be curtailed. After the Civil War, the French effort to build a transisthmian canal aroused U.S. concern, but this interest waned when the French project failed.

At the end of the nineteenth century the United States began to look beyond its borders. Construction of the Panama Canal elicited new interest in Central America. Beginning with Theodore Roosevelt and continuing through the administration of Calvin Coolidge, the United States sought to institutionalize constitutionalism and fiscal responsibility in the five countries. Intervention also provided security for the growing U.S. private interests that had invested heavily in the region. The change of U.S. policy to nonintervention during the 1930s did not alter the end result, and U.S. interests in Central America remained secure during the period of the dictators.

Following World War II, the United States became increasingly concerned with the threat of communism. While the disparity of wealth that contributed to the potential growth of communism was recognized immediately after the war, the United States failed to seriously pursue policies that might have corrected those disparities, except for two occasions: from 1961 to 1963 and again after 1979. For the most part U.S. assistance, economic and military, did little to alter the status of the ruling elite. Economic programs tended more to benefit the local elite than improve the standard of living for the poor. Military assistance tended to strengthen the institution and its alliance with the elite. Both the military and the elite viewed any alteration in the status quo as communist-inspired.

In the contemporary crisis, United States policy is a product of the past as security and stability remain the principal goal, militarily imposed if necessary. The aspirations of the middle sector and lower socio-economic groups remain of secondary interest.

Keeping the Europeans Out: The Nineteenth Century

When the Spanish American colonies sought independence, they found the United States a friendly neutral. Because the government in Washington pursued its interest in the Floridas, official support was limited to rhetoric paralleling the North American colonial experience. U.S. merchants, however, became purveyors of contraband. Spanish American agents also bought and outfitted privateers in North American waters. President James Monroe and Secretary of State John Quincy Adams successfully resisted pressures to extend recognition to the United Provinces of the Rio de la Plata (Argentina), which achieved independence in 1818. In so doing, Adams set the tone for subsequent nineteenth century U.S. policy toward its southern neighbors. There were no grounds for political affinity, and commercial relations were at best minimal.

By 1821, Spain's hold on the southern continent was tenuous, given its battlefield losses and its inability to gain European support to suppress the revolutions. These realities enabled Secretary Adams to convince President Monroe that recognition should be extended based on the fact, not the right, of independence. Recognition, it was believed, would also bring good will and aid in preserving the hemisphere from the intrigues of European diplomacy. Thus in 1822 and 1823, the United States extended recognition to Chile, Rio de Plata provinces, Peru, Colombia, and Mexico, which governed Central America at the time. In each instance, there was no prospect of independence being lost.

The second tenet of U.S. policy appeared in the 1823 Monroe Doctrine. This unilateral declaration proclaimed the western hemisphere to be republican in governmental style and closed to new European colonial expansion. European colonies already in place could remain.

When the United Provinces of Central America declared its independence from Mexico in 1824, the United States appeared aloof but did grant recognition. In 1825, the U.S. signed a commercial treaty providing for complete reciprocity, which stressed navigation rather than trade. In reality, the treaty reflected United States contacts during the colonial period. U.S. interest was transisthmian, for without

Pacific possessions it did little but dream about empire. The treaty's commercial provisions only confirmed the limited U.S. contacts with the British settlement at Belize, an important outlet for Central American produce, and the trading contacts with Indians as far south as the San Juan River.

The United Provinces insisted upon U.S. participation in the 1826 Panama congress, called by Spanish-American liberator Simon Bolívar to deal with potential foreign intruders. In the United States, northerners favored participation in order to improve commercial relations, while southerners were opposed, fearing that the slavery issue might be discussed. In Congress, the Jacksonians used the invitation to embarrass the Adams administration, causing a four month delay in appropriating funds for the delegates to go to Panama. Consequently, the Panama congress officially ended before the U.S. delegates arrived.

In his sixty-four pages of instructions to the Panama congress delegates, Richard Anderson and John Sergeant, Secretary of State Henry Clay pointed out that the U.S. would pursue a unilateral hemispheric policy and argued that there was no need for entangling alliances. He also called for trade reciprocity and reiterated the U.S. stand against transfer of territory. Further evidence of disinterest in the region's development surfaced in 1831 when Secretary of State Edward Livingston instructed newly-appointed chargé d'affaires William Jeffers not to meddle in Central American domestic affairs, but to identify only with such common causes as republicanism and complementary economics. Little materialized between the United States and Central America from 1824 to 1849. At best, the history of the eleven diplomats assigned to the region by Washington was one of futility, interspersed with comedy. The most notable was John L. Stephens, who distinguished himself for work with the Mayan ruins rather than with contemporary politics.

While the United States ignored Central America in the early 1800s, Great Britain strengthened its position there. For the British, it appeared natural for them to replace the Spanish as the dominant merchant force, subsequently claiming to be defending Great Britain's commercial interests than pursuing an aggressive policy. To the Central and North Americans, however, the British came to be viewed as neocolonials. British Foreign Minister Lord Palmerston instructed his representative to Central America from 1834 to 1852, Frederick Chatfield, to protect British nationals and preserve British commercial supremacy in the region. Chatfield's actions made him appear to be an agent of imperialism. He actively opposed Central American union, preferring to deal with the weaker independent states. He defended the British protectorate over Belize, which was based on a long list of documents detailing arrangements worked out with the Spanish during the colonial period. He also justified, as defensive, the seizure in 1838 of Raután Island off the Honduran coast.

Chatfield's activities in Nicaragua came at a time of increased U.S. interest in a transisthmian canal, an interest which was intensified by Manifest Destiny and subsequent discovery of gold in California. Nicaragua was considered the most feasible canal route with the San Juan River as its Atlantic terminus. In 1848, however, Chatfield sanctioned the establishment of a British protectorate over the Mosquito Coast, which also included the mouth of the San Juan River. The Nicaraguans had no choice but to accept it. On the Pacific side, the British seized Tigre Island in the Gulf of Fonseca, a prospective western terminus for a canal. These actions prompted Secretary of State John M. Clayton to caution against a possible collision of divergent American and British interests.

United States diplomats assigned to the region in 1848—Joseph Livingston at León, Elijah Hise at Guatemala and Ephraim G. Squier who replaced Hise in 1849—were instructed to check British advances by encouraging the reestablishment of the Central American federation. Hise exceeded his instructions when negotiating friendship treaties with Nicaragua, Honduras and El Salvador. The Nicaraguan treaty also granted the United States the perpetual right to build and fortify a canal across Nicaragua in return for a pledge to protect Nicaraguan territory. None of the treaties was ever submitted to congress, and Squier replaced Hise following Zachary Taylor's inauguration.

Squier was equally desirous of a canal connecting U.S. coastlines. He struck with quick success. In September 1849 he reached an agreement with Nicaragua for construction and protection of a canal, and with Honduras for the cession of Tigre Island. This action prompted the British seizure of the island in October, with Chatfield citing a "lien" he had levied on the island the previous January.

Secretary Clayton, who had favored a canal open to all nations and unencumbered by special interests, used the Hise and Squier treaties to force a British retreat. Lord Palmerston was equally willing to avoid confrontation. The upshot was the 1850 Clayton-Bulwer Treaty, whereby each major power agreed to cooperate in facilitating the construction of a nonfortified isthmian canal. The treaty was less precise regarding territorial interests in Central America. The negotiators agreed to ambiguous language in Article I, so as to conceal official differences. The article provided that neither country would "occupy," or "colonize," or exercise "dominion" over any part of Central America, a region deliberately not defined by the treaty. The North Americans interpreted this to mean that Britain would abandon its occupied territories, while the British interpreted the article to mean that they would not expand beyond their current holdings.

For the decade following the Clayton-Bulwer Treaty, the United States and Great Britain continued to haggle over the interpretation of Article I. In response to a British effort to collect harbor fees from a private U.S. merchant ship at Greytown in 1851, the American navy made a show of force, which brought a British apology. Three years later, U.S. naval forces set fire to the town in response to intimidation of American citizens by local desperadoes. Diplomatic discussions regarding British control over the Bay Island was expanded to include Belize. In 1853, Secretary of State William L. Marcy unsuccessfully attempted to have the British abandon Raután Island under the provisions of Article I. Finally, a series of agreements between 1856 and 1860 clearly defined the British sphere of influence. These settlements defined the Belize boundary, made the Bay Islands a free territory under Honduran jurisdiction, and granted the Mosquito territory autonomy under British protection, and compensation from Nicaragua. President James Buchanan expressed satisfaction that Britain's interest in Central America had been restricted. One of the Monroe Doctrine's proclamations had been fulfilled.

To the British, William Walker's three expeditions into Central America in 1855, 1857, and 1860 appeared as the advance guard of Manifest Destiny. They accused Walker of secretly trying to acquire Central American territory for the United States, a clear violation of the Clayton-Bulwer Treaty. U.S. failure to enforce its antifilibustering laws strengthened this opinion. Walker's death before a Honduran firing squad in 1860 finally put the issue to rest.

With the Civil War and Reconstruction, and the subsequent movement westward to the Pacific Coast, foreign policy was not in the forefront of the national political arena. Central American issues became even less important, although concern with European expansion there remained. Americans protested the Spanish reoccupation of the Dominican Republic in 1861 and, with copies to the five Central American nations, warned Madrid that further encroachments would be met with resistance. The Spanish withdrew in 1865 due to local resistance, not U.S. pressure.

British interests in Central America remained an irritant. Although mahogany markets dwindled in the late 1800s, the British refused to abandon Belize declaring it British Honduras in 1862 with a lieutenant governor responsible to the governor of Jamaica. Its continued occupation of the Mosquito Coast proved more troublesome. The Nicaraguan government sought U.S. support of their demand that the British abandon its protectorate over the territory. While Britain claimed that the government in Managua had little interest in the Indians of the Mosquito Coast, the Nicaraguans charged that the British occupation hampered progress toward an isthmian canal. European affairs, rather than Nicaraguan efforts, largely contributed to the British abandonment of its protectorate over the Mosquito Coast in 1895, enabling the Nicaraguans to proclaim their sovereignty over the Indians, thus ending a long-standing dispute.

The prospect of a transisthmian canal periodically affected U.S. policy towards Central America after the Civil War. In 1867, President Andrew Johnson suggested that the United States guarantee a Nicaraguan canal without violating the British prerogative under the Clayton-Bulwer Treaty. However Congress, mired in Reconstruction, was in no mood for expansion. Interest in a canal reached new heights in 1876 when President Ulysses S. Grant's Interoceanic Canal Commission recommended a route through Nicaragua. By this time, the Central Americans were cool to the proposal.

In 1879 the aging Frenchman, Ferdinand de Lesseps, builder of the Suez Canal, began developing plans for a transisthmian canal, which prompted President Rutherford B. Hayes to declare that any such canal should be under U.S. control. The American press viewed Hayes' assertion as a reaffirmation of the Monroe Doctrine, and before the year ended both houses of Congress protested against any canal being built by foreign capital or controlled by foreign corporations. The U.S. government-owned Maritime Canal Company was formed and it recommended the Nicaraguan route. The Americans,however, were more concerned with domestic affairs. This general lack of interest, coupled with the failure of the de Lesseps project, caused the canal issue to fade into the background to await a new burst of U.S. expansionism at the century's end.

Relating to its own experience, the United States favored the idea of a Central American Union in the last quarter of the nineteenth century. In 1872, Secretary of State Hamilton Fish encouraged the U.S. Minister to Nicaragua, Charles N. Riotte, to lend his support to the liberal plan for unity. Thirteen years later, in 1885, Secretary of State Thomas Bayard reiterated U.S. policy favoring a union, but not one brought about by military force as sought by Guatemalan leader Justo Rufino Barrios. In anticipation of a conflict, the United States sent five warships to the Caribbean coast, ostensibly to protect

American life and property, while the U.S. Minister to Guatemala, Henry C. Hall, labored unsuccessfully to prevent war. When Barrios died in battle, so too did the plan for union.

The United States again looked favorably upon union in 1895 when Nicaraguan dictator José Santos Zelaya brought Honduras and El Salvador into a loose confederation called the Greater Republic of Central America. On Christmas Eve in 1896, President Grover Cleveland received José Dolores Rodríguez as the Republic's Minister, the first time in fifty years that a single individual was recognized in Washington as the representative of a group of Central American states. Recognition was short lived, however, as the new president, William McKinley determined that the Republic was an association, not a federation. Thereafter, United States interests in Central America intensified and so did its attitude about union.

In the nineteenth century, the United States was drawn to Central America only when European interests there threatened to expand. The Monroe Doctrine, the Clayton-Bulwer Treaty, and post-Civil War isthmian canal excitement were simply responses to European expansion. The United States exhibited no territorial ambitions and little economic activity.

The Search for Stability: 1900-1948

In the 1880s several factors influenced the development of a new U.S. attitude. Economic considerations came first, followed by an altruistic crusade to uplift so-called "inferior" people. Strategic interests developed as a result of the Spanish-American war and the subsequent construction of the Panama Canal. Through 1915, presidential policies differed. Theodore Roosevelt's "corollary" to the Monroe Doctrine provided a moral mandate to intervene in the internal affairs of the Caribbean nations. Sympathetic to big business interests, President William Howard Taft let "Dollar Diplomacy" replace Roosevelt's "Big Stick." President Woodrow Wilson, an outspoken foe of imperialism, vehemently criticized Taft's "Dollar Diplomacy," yet intervened in Latin America more than any of his predecessors. Although policies differed, the objective remained the same—U.S. supremacy over the region.

Construction of the Panama Canal significantly influenced U.S. policy toward Central America. Abrogation of the Clayton-Bulwer Treaty in 1901 removed the British as an obstacle to U.S. construction of a transisthmian canal. There was intense political manuevering within the United States over where to build the canal, Nicaragua or Panama, the latter still a province of Colombia in 1901. Finally in June 1902 congress authorized the president to secure the Panama route from Colombia. The government in Bogotá, however, rejected the Hay-Herran Treaty. The Panamanians, long desirous of independence now found a sympathetic ear in Washington. Revolution followed in November 1903. The United States quickly recognized Panama's independence and completed the Hay-Bunau-Varilla Treaty, by which the United States received the right to construct and maintain a canal across Panama. Construction began immediately. The canal opened to world commerce in 1914, just prior to the outbreak of World War I.

Because of the canal, the United States took greater interest in Central American affairs. U.S. policymakers viewed political and financial instability in the region as potentially disruptive to Panama, and also as potential cause for European intervention. In either instance, the canal's security was threatened and contributed to the U.S. desire for political stability in Central America. In Washington, a conscious effort emerged to impose constitutional government throughout Central America.

The United States first intervened under the banner of constitutionalism in 1906, when, with the Mexican government, it negotiated an end to the Guatemalan-Honduran/Salvadoran conflict. War again threatened the region in 1907, when Nicaraguan President José Santos Zelaya attempted to extend his influence over Honduras and El Salvador. The United States and Mexico offered to mediate, resulting in the 1907 Washington Conference, which sought to settle all outstanding difficulties and to establish Central American relations on a permanently peaceful basis.

After defeating Honduran and Nicaraguan efforts to discuss political union, the Washington Conference produced several conventions. The three most important were a ten year General Treaty of Peace and Amity; a Central American Court of Justice; and a Central American Bureau. The general peace treaty recognized the U.S. ideals of constitutionalism and respect for national integrity by providing for the nonrecognition of any government which came to power by a coup d'etat or revolution. In addition, it called for nonintervention in the internal affairs of other states and for constitutional provisions regulating the re-election of presidents. The Court of Justice was envisioned as a non-political tool to settle disputes among the five nations. The Central American Bureau was commissioned to (1) introduce modern education facilities, (2) develop trade, agriculture and industry, and (3) reform legal institutions.

While the Bureau was not an instrument of political union, there was hope that at least it would increase regional cooperation.

For the next decade, the United States based its policy toward Central America on the principles established at the 1907 conference. Dana G. Munro, of the State Department's Latin American Affairs Division, noted that the energetic U.S. insistence these principles practically put an end to the wars that had plagued Central America.

For its part, the United States did not comply with these same agreements. While the U.S. was seeking to keep the Central Americans from interfering in each other's affairs, it failed to pursue a similar policy. Intervention took many forms. Secretary of State Philander C. Knox told the Senate Foreign Relations Committee that U.S. capital would be a significant instrument in bringing stability to the neighborhood of the Panama Canal. For that reason the State Department became involved in the refinancing, by U.S. private banks, of Costa Rican, Honduran, Guatemalan and Nicaraguan international debts. When Zelaya was confronted with a revolution in 1909, the United States justified military intervention as assistance to the Nicaraguans in their desire for peace and prosperity under constitutional government.

U.S. Minister to Honduras, Thomas C. Dawson, personally selected Francisco Bertrand as Honduran provisional president in 1913, bringing an end to two years of civil war. Recognition was withheld from Frederico Tinoco when he seized power in Costa Rica in 1917. Finally, the United States contributed to the demise of the Central American Court of Justice. Certain provisions of the 1914 Bryan-Chamorro Treaty, which granted the U.S. rights to build a canal through Nicaragua, were viewed as an infringement of Salvadoran rights in the Gulf of Fonseca and Costa Rican rights on the San Juan River. The court ruled in their favor in 1916 and 1917, but the United States ignored the decisions. In 1918, no efforts were made to renew the 1907 convention establishing the court.

When political intrigue again unsettled the region in 1920 and 1921, the State Department's Latin American Affairs Division insisted that the 1907 treaties were still in affect. Not until 1922, however, when war threatened, was Division Chief Francis G. White able to persuade Secretary of State Charles Evans Hughes to convene a conference to deal with Central American political instability. The Division favored a Central American union, believing that it would contribute to stability, facilitate investment, and limit Mexican influence. (The United States had not yet entended recognition to Mexico following its revolution.) Hughes rejected this advice, asserting that the region's history militated against any cooperative effort.

Hughes avoided the issue in the conference invitation to the participating countries, and at the intial session he emphatically advised the
delegates that union was not to be a topic of discussion. Hughes was
concerned more with accomplishing political stability through
specific agreements.

When the conference adjourned February 7, 1923, twelve agreements were signed. Five fell within the purview of United States
objectives to improve Central American peace and stability: (1)
General Treaty of Peace and Amity; (2) establishment of an International Commission of Inquiry (the only agreement signed by the
United States); (3) establishment of an International Central American Tribunal; (4) projects of Electoral Legislation; and (5) an Arms
Limitation Convention.

The provisions of the General Treaty of Peace and Amity expanded upon those in the 1907 convention. The nonrecognition of
revolutionary governments, rebel leaders, or their relatives was
designed to discourage coups d'etat, and the agreement not to harbor
foreign revolutionary groups was to assist in preventing liberal or
conservative exiles from plotting a forceful return to power.

Disputes between the five countries were to be settled peacefully,
utilizing a new International Central American Tribunal and Commission of Inquiry. Unlike the court established in 1907, the new
court would have permanent justices. The inquiry commission would
issue non-binding reports on disputes, including recommended solutions.

The Electoral Legislation projects called for the establishment of a
Central American Commission of Jurists to codify voting procedures, equal representation on electoral boards, classification of
political parties, and verification of voting returns. These first four
conventions were within the U.S. objective of maintaining regional
stability through recognition of constitutional order. All four conventions were to be effective until January 1, 1934.

The United States was confident that arms reduction in Central
America would alleviate interference in domestic political affairs of
neighbor states, remove an arbitrary source of domestic political
power, and relieve each nation from excessive military budgets.
Although all five Central American nations agreed in principle to
arms reduction, each was preoccupied with its own concerns, based
on considerations of population, area, military strength, internal
order and border defense. While the United States favored the replacement of standing armies with constabularies or national guards,
not all agreed, particularly Salvador. However, the United States
achieved its objectives in the final Arms LimitationConvention. The

size of each nation's standing army, including a national guard was fixed for a five year period: Guatemala 5200; El Salvador 4200; Honduras 2500; Nicaragua 2500; and Costa Rica 2000 men, each.

Secretary Hughes considered the 1923 conventions an improvement over the 1907 agreements in contributing to the region's tranquility, and that they served the interests of both the Central American countries and the United States. The general peace treaty strengthened constitutionalism by broadening the grounds for non-recognition. Hughes was cautious, however, believing that since elections often were meaningless, coups d'etat were about the only measures available to dislodge corrupt governments. On this basis, he reasoned, one could argue that the Central Americans were entitled to their revolutions. The United States, however, could not tolerate any disturbance in the Caribbean region that would affect the security of the Panama Canal. Yet, Hughes hoped that these treaties would prevent revolutions that could result in regional anarchy.

Hughes also believed that other agreements reached at the conference furthered the cause of Central American stability. The Central American Tribunal was considered an improvement over the Central American Court of Justice, since the selected justices would be of improved quality and not subject to nationalistic pressures. The Commission of Inquiry was designed to respond quickly to treaty violations so as to facilitate the settlement of disputes. United States participation supposedly would expedite investigations and reports. The Electoral Legislation projects were considered a step toward expanding the free exercise of popular suffrage. Finally, the arms limitation agreement would provide practical benefits to local economies and potentially reduce the military's political role. Hughes concluded that these five agreements constituted a distinct advance in the prevention of revolutionary disturbances and a contribution to Central American stability and prosperity. He instructed U.S. ministers in each Central American country to exert their influence to procure ratification.

These five agreements met varied fates. Only two—Peace and Amity and Arms Limitation—were ratified by all Central American governments. El Salvador refused to ratify Article II of the Peace and Amity Treaty, which detailed the nonrecognition of governments coming to power by other than constitutional means. Salvador also rejected the agreement establishing a Tribunal, and Costa Rica the one creating an Inquiry Commission. Only Nicaragua and Honduras approved the Electoral Reform pact.

The 1923 treaties continued the policies the United States had pursued toward Central America since 1900—the assumption of responsibility for regional political order. Yet while Washington's policymakers considered the 1923 treaties a distinct improvement over those concluded in 1907, the response of the Central American legislatures to the 1923 treaties, should have been seen as an omen. Until 1932, only Costa Rica escaped political turmoil and U.S. intervention.

In Honduras, prior to the October 1923 presidential election, U.S. Minister Frank T. Morales failed in his efforts to have all factions agree on a compromise candidate. Secretary Hughes dismissed a Guatemalan proposal for a conference, believing that regional liberal and conservative governments would support their respective groups in Honduras. When revolution erupted following the elections, the United States landed Marines ostensibly to protect American lives and property. Sumner Welles was dispatched to work out a solution, which provided that liberal Vincente Tosta, not in violation of the 1923 treaty, serve as provisional president until new elections were held in 1924. Tiburcio Carías, knowing that recognition would be denied if he seized office, put his aspirations aside until 1932 when he captured the presidency through the ballot box.

After World War I, United States interest in Nicaragua waned to the point where Secretary Hughes instructed the withdrawal of U.S. Marines following the 1924 presidential election. When Emiliano Chamorro forced President Carlos Solórzano from office, the U.S. withheld recognition on the basis of the 1923 treaty. Again U.S. Marines landed to protect American lives and property, and Henry L. Stimson was sent to work out a solution. This included U.S. Marine supervision of the 1928 election won by liberal José Maria Moncada. The State Department stretched its interpretation of the 1923 treaty to justify Moncada's eligibility. As it had some fifteen years before, the United States again imposed order, violating, if not the text, at least the spirit of the 1907 and 1923 treaties.

In Guatemala, General Manuel Orellana came to power in December 1930 through a coup, in clear violation of the 1923 treaty. The United States withheld recognition and persuaded the other Central American nations to do the same. On instructions from Washington, Minister Sheldon Whitehouse labored for restoration of constitutional government. The 1934 election of Jorge Ubico, who ran unopposed, accomplished this. Not identified with the Orellana revolt, Ubico was quickly granted recognition.

A 1931 revolt in El Salvador forced the ouster of President Arturo Araujo. Although there was no clear evidence that General Maximiliano Hernández Martínez was associated with the revolt, U.S. Minister to San Salvador, Charles Curtis, determined that the Hernández regime was not entitled to recognition under the terms of the

1923 treaty. Hernández weathered the storm and, when the Central American countries permitted the 1923 treaty to expire, the United States began pursuing a new policy toward the region. In 1935, Washington followed the other Central American governments in extending recognition.

The effort to impose constitutional government upon Central America failed, as did the five 1923 agreements considered important by the United States. With the exception of Costa Rica, military expenditures were not reduced, and only Honduras reported a military establishment within the treaty limits. Guatemala maintained an army larger than allocated. Both Salvador and Nicaragua created national guards but in the former, the guard was in addition to the army. In Nicaragua the National Guard took on the characteristics of an army in pursuit of rebels led by Augusto C. Sandino. The Central American Tribunal convened only once, while the Commission of Inquiry and Electoral Legislation projects were never instituted. The traditional pattern of political dynamics remained.

During the 1920s evidence of new U.S. policy directions began to mount. The 1924 Democratic Party platform included a plank opposing direct intervention and promoting inter-American goodwill. In 1926, State Department official Stokely W. Morgan suggested that the United States let local revolutionaries "fight it out." Writing in *Foreign Affairs* in 1928, Franklin D. Roosevelt criticized unilateral intervention and President-elect Herbert Hoover espoused the same principles during a goodwill tour of Latin America. Successive heads of the Latin American Affairs Division, Francis G. White and Edwin C. Wilson, also believed that it was no longer necessary to extend unwelcomed protection or to meddle in Central American affairs. Intervention in Latin American domestic affairs was first criticized in Under Secretary of State's J. Reuben Clark's *Memorandum on the Monroe Doctrine* which detached the Roosevelt Corollary from the Monroe Doctrine. All three views signaled a change in U.S. policy, if not objectives, and was announced as the Good Neighbor Policy by President Franklin D. Roosevelt in his 1933 inaugural address.

The new policy was evident in the attitude of the United States toward the 1934 Central American Conference in Guatemala City, which brought an end to the 1923 treaty system. At three Inter-American conferences during the 1930s—Montevideo, 1933; Buenos Aires, 1936; and Lima, 1938—the United States pledged not to interfere directly or indirectly in the domestic concerns of Latin America and to abandon nonrecognition as a diplomatic device to change governments.

A new government seeking U.S. recognition now had to meet three criteria; it had to (1) control the nation's territory and administrative machinery, including maintenance of public order; (2) be able to meet its international obligations, and (3) have the willing support of the populace. From 1935 to 1944, Central American dictators Hernández in El Salvador, Ubico in Guatemala, Carías in Honduras, and Somoza in Nicaragua met the new criteria each time they extended their stay in office. Thus, the new policy permitted the dictators to secure themselves in power.

In February 1944, Under Secretary of State Edward R. Stettinius cautioned the U.S. missions in the region to be prepared for political turmoil. He advised each ambassador to avoid any act that could be interpreted as interference in local political situations. Until 1949, U.S. ambassadors avoided any role in the upheavals that followed except for Ambassador Nathaniel P. Davis, who was requested to act as a courier and mediator between the feuding factions in the 1948 Costa Rican civil war. Although the diplomats avoided direct involvement, privately each continually expressed the U.S. preference for constitutional government.

On five occasions between 1944 and 1947 U.S. policymakers were confronted with the recognition issue. Three leaders whose governments were judged to meet the criteria were granted recognition: General Andres Menéndez, who replaced Hernández in El Salvador in May 1944; General Federico Ponce, who replaced Ubico in Guatemala in July 1944; and the junta that replaced Ponce in October of the same year.

When Salvadoran Colonel Osmín Aguirre y Salinas replaced Menéndez in October he was in violation of the existing constitution and reportedly had no popular support. Unopposed, General Salvador Castaneda Castro won the February 1945 presidential election, but failed to convince Ambassador John F. Simmons that it was an expression of the Salvadoran popular will. Secretary of State Stettinius, however, anxious to present hemisphere solidarity at the forthcoming Mexico City Conference, seized the opportunity and extended recognition to the Castaneda regime. Idealism gave way to political necessity.

Finally, Somoza's 1947 political manueverings in Nicaragua resulted in U. S. nonrecognition of the presidencies of Benjamin Lucayo Sacasa and Victor Manuel Ramón y Reyes. Latin American nations followed the U.S. lead until the Ninth Inter-American Conference at Bogotá in March 1948. The conference passed a resolution denouncing nonrecognition as a political tool. The U.S. supported the resolution for several reasons. Former ministers to Latin American nations, study groups within the State Department, and such eminent scholars as John Bassett Moore, Charles Chevy Hyde, Raymond L. Buell and Samuel Flagg Bemis all indicated that nonrecognition amounted to nothing more than an expression of displeasure with the government in question. Many Latin nations wanted to keep the United States from interfering in the domestic affairs of their hemispheric neighbors, and there was an evident desire for a demonstration of hemispheric solidarity at the conference. The weight of the majority opinion was persuasive, and the U.S. delegation accepted the resolution. The Nicaraguan government was quickly granted recognition, marking the end to another era of U.S. policy toward Central America.

The central theme of U.S. policy towards Central America in the first half of the twentieth century was a desire for political tranquility prompted by the need for security of the Panama Canal. It resulted in direct intervention in efforts to force constitutional government on the Central American countries. From this perspective, the 1923 Washington Conference was a high water mark. The futility of the policy, however, contributed to nonintervention after 1933. The North Americans, if not content, were at least indifferent toward the dictatorships that followed. At the same time they ignored the middle sector demands for democratic government and the lower socioeconomic groups' need for improved living standards.

Central American political stability also provided security for the expanding U.S. private investments that replaced the Europeans as the dominant force in the agricultural, banking, and commercial sectors in each of the five nations. Political stability, however defined, also secured U.S. private businesses, which shared their government's indifference toward the demands of the middle sector and lower socioeconomic groups.

The Communists are Coming: 1945-1976

The overriding objective of U.S. foreign policy since 1945 has been the containment of communism. At first, global strategy sought to deter Soviet expansion in Europe, Communist China in Asia, and subsequently communist influence in Third World areas. Policy toward Latin America followed the contours of global patterns. The Act of Chapultepec adopted at the Mexico City conference in 1945, the defense agreements reached at the Rio de Janiero conference in 1947, the creation of the Inter-American Defense Board at Bogota in

1948, and passage of the Military Security Act in 1951 demonstrated the United States' concern with an external attack on the hemisphere, presumably communist. At the Tenth Inter-American Conference of American States, meeting in Caracas, Venezuela in March 1954, the United States pushed through a resolution asserting that the subjection of any American nation to communist political control was considered foreign intervention and a threat to the peace of the Americas. Communists, however identified, were considered agents of the Soviet Union and therefore linked to the international conspiracy against the United States. Fidel Castro's successful revolution in Cuba brought new considerations. Concerned that communism's appeal to the disenfranchised and poverty stricken masses might spread, the United States introduced the Alliance for Progress. At the same time, Washington redesigned military assistance to meet the communist internal threat. Central America became a microcosm of these larger issues.

The communist issue first emerged in Central America during the early Cold War years, from 1944 to 1949. American diplomats in the field admittedly were unable to judge the opinions of the lower socioeconomic classes, which were considered the targets of communist propaganda. In three countries—El Salvador, Honduras, and Nicaragua—U.S. diplomats believed communist organizations to be almost non-existent. In all three, communist parties were outlawed, and any contact with communists was through Mexico. After 1947, field reports expressed concern that poverty provided a breeding ground for communism, and that potentially the region was of importance to the Soviet Union. Still, U.S. policymakers considered communism to be of local character only.

In Costa Rica and Guatemala, however, communism took on a different character. Communism in Costa Rica began in 1931 when Manuel Mora founded the local Communist Party. The party championed the cause of the lower class and reached the height of its popularity in 1944, when it significantly contributed to the election of Teodoro Picado. Charges by the upper class that communism was threatening the nation were dismissed by U.S. officials, who concluded that the party was of local character only, had no direct ties to Moscow, and that its programs would be described as liberal in most countries. After 1947, the party became increasingly isolated, but it also became more militant and remained the only voice of the lower class. Diplomats in the field understood this, but with the stiffening U.S. attitude towards the Soviet Union, they suggested Costa Rica's potential importance as a regional message and training center to the Soviets. The outlawing of the Communist Party following the 1948 civil war was justified by José Figueres' claim that the war saved the country from communism, a claim Ambassador Nathaniel P. Davis found difficult to accept. Rather, Davis viewed communism as an issue the local elite exploited to preserve its position; moreover, he found the economic and social philosophies of both Mora and Figueres strikingly similar.

More significant were the events in Guatemala. At the time of Ubico's overthrow in Guatemala in 1944, U.S. policy makers concluded that there was no communist activity in the country despite the vast poverty among the Indians tied to the nation's large agricultural holdings. Following the election of Juan José Arévalo in 1945, the question of communist influence in government surfaced. Given Arévalo's philosophy and legislative program, the elite charged that he was a communist and that he appointed communists to government posts. With the exception of Assistant Secretary of State Spruille Braden, who was convinced that Arévalo was a communist and had a secret agreement with Josef Stalin, most U.S. officials did not find a Moscow connection. True, communists had infiltrated the Guatemalan government, but as late as 1949 the State Department's Office of Intelligence Research could not confirm any Soviet connection.

Occupied with communist aggression in Europe and Asia, and perceiving no immediate Soviet threat to Central America, the United States largely ignored the region during the early Cold War period. For most U.S. policymakers, the communist issue was understood to be an instrument used by the elite to maintain its privileged status.

Following the election of President Dwight D. Eisenhower in 1952, the communist issue in Central America took on new meaning, particularly in Guatemala where President Jacobo Arbenz struck directly at the large landowners. In June 1952 he announced a government plan to expropriate controlled land above a certain acreage for distribution to the peasants. Landowners were to be compensated in bonds. Under the program, some 1.5 million acres were taken with compensation at $8.4 million. To some Americans, and many Guatemalans the program did not appear punitive.

Guatemalan landowners and UFCO, which lost 234,000 acres, viewed the program as a communist scheme. The number of Marxist oriented labor leaders and government bureaucrats, coupled with Guatemala's pro-Soviet path at the United Nations, was enough to convince Secretary of State John Foster Dulles that a Soviet satellite was emerging in Central America. In 1953, a Central Intelligence Agency (CIA) estimate predicted the strengthening of the communist hand in Guatemala and potentially elsewhere in the region.

These factors contributed to the Dulles-sponsored anticommunist resolution at the Caracas Inter-American Conference in 1954.

These same factors also resulted in U.S. support, through the CIA, for Colonel Castillo Armas and General Miguel Ydĩgoras Fuentes, who were plotting a revolution against Arbenz. Senior and conservative military officers within Guatemala were disturbed by events within the country and by Arbenz' plan to create a new armed force. They found a friend in Ambassador John Puerifoy who was more than observer to the generals' demand that Arbenz resign in June 1954. At the same time Castillo's army of 168 men invaded the country and at Puerifoy's insistence, he assumed control of the government.

The Guatemalan affair set in motion plans for incorporating Central America into hemispheric defense plans. Under the provisions of the 1951 Mutual Security Act, the United States reached Military Defense Assistance Pacts with Guatemala, Honduras, and Nicaragua. By 1959, there were U.S. Army missions in all the Central American countries and U.S. Air Force missions in all but Costa Rica.

Under the terms of these programs, the recipient nations were to improve and expand their armed forces with surplus U.S. military equipment, mostly of World War II origin. The stated objective was to secure the hemisphere against external aggression. Central America's role stressed the security of the Panama Canal, and Mexican and Venezuelan oil. To receive assistance, the recipient government had only to support U.S. foreign policy and oppose communism. This arrangement resulted in indiscriminate aid packages during the 1950s that seemed to strengthen the dictators at the expense of constitutional government and social reform throughout Central America.

The emphasis on military solutions to regional problems during the Eisenhower administration was illustrated again in November 1960 when the United States sent warships, without OAS approval, along the Guatemalan and Nicaraguan coast to guard against a possible Cuban attack. Moreover, the Eisenhower administration ignored the concepts of mutual defense and collective security, as found in the 1947 Rio Pact and 1948 OAS Charter, when it trained Cuban exiles for the Bay of Pigs invasion. The fear of a monolithic communist conspiracy predicated the administration's actions.

President John F. Kennedy offered a new approach to the military assistance policy. He believed that the success of Castro's revolution would encourage similar movements against other dictators. To ward off such possibilities, Kennedy based the provision of U.S. military assistance on a recipient government's willingness to promote political and social reform. The first application of the new policy occurred in early 1961 when recognition was withheld from the Salvadoran military junta until it promised to hold elections and return to constitutional government.

In 1961 the Foreign Assistance Act replaced the 1954 Mutual Security Act. The new program provided military assistance to stem both internal and external aggression. The Central American military was now to be prepared for internal security. This meant an emphasis on lightweight and mobile equipment instead of heavy matériel, and training in the art of counterinsurgency warfare. Kennedy also accepted a recommendation to train the military to implement constructive civil action programs—the building of roads, bridges, hospitals, and so forth. The purpose was to improve the public image of the local military.

The new policy failed to bring about the anticipated results. The military often moved against any group described as "left," or in some cases, notably Guatemala, military personnel trained in anti-guerrilla tactics became guerrillas themselves. The few civic action programs did little to improve the long tarnished image of the military. Furthermore the the civic action programs received only 15.6% of the U.S. military appropriations, while 56.6% was earmarked for internal security, suggesting to critics that the United States had little real interest in reform. Criticism of Kennedy's policy significantly contributed to his withholding of recognition of the López Arenallo junta in Honduras in November 1963. Aid was halted and all military advisors and personnel withdrawn. The result of Kennedy's actions remain speculative because of his death and the subsequent policy redirection by President Lyndon Johnson. Two months after assuming the presidency, Johnson extended recognition to Honduras and restored all aid programs, an indication that his administration would not pressure military regimes.

Johnson's policy was more clearly defined in March 1964 by Thomas C. Mann, Assistant Secretary of State for Latin American Affairs. Mann explained that the United States, while continuing to pursue political democracy for Latin America, intended to display a greater concern with U.S. national security and investments by thwarting communist expansion. This meant intensified training of the military and police to meet communist subversion. Critics of the Mann Doctrine quickly pointed out that the United States was reverting to a policy indiscriminate assistance to military regimes that had been followed during the Eisenhower administration.

TABLE V

United States Military Assistance
to Central America
(millions of dollars)

	Mutual Security Pact 1953-1961	Foreign Assistance Act 1962-1969	Nixon/Ford 1970-1976	Carter 1977-1981	Reagan 1982-1984
Costa Rica	0.1	1.7	0.0	0.0	59.3
El Salvador	0.1	6.5	4.2	41.4	107.8
Guatemala	1.5	17.9	21.6	0.0	148.1
Honduras	1.1	8.0	7.7	18.3	172.3
Nicaragua	1.9	10.4	16.8	0.4	0.0
Totals	4.7	44.5	50.3	60.1	487.5

Source: Agency for International Development, **Overseas Loans and Grants and Assistance from International Organizations**, July 1945 - September 1981, pp. 43, 47, 48 and 54. Agency for International Development, **Congressional Presentation, FY1984, Annex III, Latin America,** (includes estimates), pp. 87, 138, 153, 201 and 221.

Johnson maintained Kennedy's military arrangements which emphasized lightweight weapons and mobile assistance, continued military training in U.S. camps, and maintained civic action programs. In 1967, however, Congress curtailed the amount of overall military assistance by placing a dollar limit on the military aid programs. The total value of defense articles furnished to Latin America was set at $100 million annually, and the amount of arms furnished at $75 million annually. Congress may have had second thoughts about propping up dictatorships, but more likely it was influenced by the cost of the Vietnam War. By 1970, overall U.S. military personnel in Latin America had declined by 35% of its 1967 level. undeterred, however, the local military establishment now turned to European arms merchants.

President Richard M. Nixon reversed Johnson's military policy toward Latin America. In 1969, Nixon endorsed Nelson A. Rockefeller's report on Latin America, which called for continuation of military aid to combat communism, and did not discourage recognition of unconstitutional governments. Beginning in 1971 Nixon successfully persuaded congress to raise the 1967 ceilings to $150 million, and in October 1974 succeeded in having the limit on credit extended to Latin American countries suspended altogether. Critics observed, and government officials admitted, that the arms sales represented an effort to recoup monies lost since 1967. The sale of $6.5 million worth of military equipment to Guatemala in 1972 netted the United States an approximate $3.5 million in excess of the total amount of military grants it made to Central America for the same year. "Defense" was becoming a secondary consideration. The granting of recognition to López Arenallo, who again seized the Honduran presidency in 1972, demonstrated the lack of concern with political reform.

United States military assistance to the five Central American countries is detailed in Table V. The figures reflect the variable trends in overall military policy toward Latin America, rather than support the allegation that the United Stated fostered militarism in the region. For example, while overall expenditures to Latin America decreased from 1967 to 1970, those for Central America remained constant. This was because of the concern with internal security of the isthmus and the belief that military assistance had a greater impact on smaller countries than on larger ones.

Consistently, the U.S. government denied responsibilities for fostering Central American militarism, insisting instead that the U.S. objective remained constant: to stop the spread of communism in the region. By design or not, however, U.S. military policy certainly did not reduce the importance of the military as the bulwark of government in Central America. The number of Central American troops trained by the United States (Table VI) and the close relationship between the U.S. military missions and the local officer corps in each country, led to several damning allegations. For example, the military coups and authoritarian repression in Honduras and Guatemala in the late 1960s and early 1970s could not have occurred without the knowledge of the U.S. military missions in Tegucigalpa and Guatemala City. Also, Central American officers sought to improve their own living standards. To this end, many pursued private economic activities or profitable government posts, increasing their desire to maintain the status quo.

The U.S. training of the Central American military included efforts to influence the political thinking of the soldiers. The emphasis was on the evils of communism. In 1970 the Southern Command, headquartered in Panama and responsible for the security of Central America, described a communist government as one run by a small group of individuals for their own benefit, while pretending to benefit peasants and labor. State control of the economy was presented as concomitant with repression of individual freedoms. These concepts appeared to parallel the arguments put forward by the elite in support of the status quo. Whatever the impact of this feature of their training, the fact is that the Central American military, except in Costa Rica, has moved with increasing intensity against all groups and individuals advocating any drastic changes in the socioeconomic structure.

TABLE VI

Central American Soliders Trained
by the U.S. Under MAP, 1950-1972

	Trained in U.S.	Trained in Canal Zone	Total
Costa Rica	33	496	529
El Salvador	200	1,077	1,277
Guatemala	656	1,920	2,576
Honduras	221	1,791	2,012
Nicaragua	693	3,704	4,397
Regional Totals	1803	9,988	10,791

Source: U.S. Department of Defense, **Military Assistance Pacts 1973**, p.194.

The argument that U.S. military policy entrenched the Central American dictators, with the exception of Costa Rica, has found support in its social and economic policies. Foreign Service officers during the Truman administration correctly observed that poverty served as breeding ground for communism. Economic assistance in Central America during the Truman administration totaled $26.9 million (Table VII), an amount insufficient to deal with the magnitude of the poverty problem.

The Eisenhower-Dulles team used bold rhetoric regarding Latin America's needs. They castigated Truman for ignoring the hemisphere's social and economic problems. Hope for new directions in Latin American policy was provided in Milton Eisenhower's *Report on Latin America* and the Randall Commission's study, *Foreign Economic Policy*, both issued in late 1953. Both documents argued for a more liberal U.S. trade policy through tariff reductions and a need to assist in providing basic social services for the poor. These recommendations were in sharp contrast to the ideas of Eisenhower's closest advisors, businessmen who were advocates of private enterprise, a sharp contrast to Latin American reformers advocating increased state activity in the region's social and economic spheres. Rather than following the advice of the Milton Eisenhower and Randall Commission reports, the Latin American governments were advised to create an environment conducive to private investment; and when accomplished, U.S. dollars would follow to support the necessary infrastructure.

Economic assistance to Central America totaled $253.4 million during the Eisenhower administration, a nine-fold increase over the Truman years (Table VII). The total is deceiving. Approximately half went to Guatemala in response to 1954 Armas invasion. Also the terms under which the aid was received reflected the management concepts of Eisenhower's advisors. The United States assumed the high initial costs for technical assistance with the host countries agreeing to eventually assume 66% of the total cost. For the Central American governments, this proved a difficult task. The amount of money lost to high administrative costs and possible corruption only complicated their ability to meet financial obligations. Moreover the region's agricultural exports depended on fluctuating world market prices and were at the mercy of tariffs imposed by the United States, which was the largest importer of region's goods. By 1961, there was no measurable improvement in the region's economy or social conditions.

Latin American frustration with the failure of U.S. policy to meet its economic and social needs during the 1950s, became apparant

TABLE VII

United States Economic Assistance
to Central America
(millions of dollars)

	Truman Administration	Eisenhower Administration	Kennedy/ Johnson Administrations	Nixon/Ford Administrations	Carter Administration	Reagan Administration
Costa Rica	6.0	52.1	101.1	58.6	58.3	258.0
El Salvador	2.3	11.1	105.8	49.3	194.6	505.3
Guatemala	9.9	121.3	93.7	139.8	67.3	125.7
Honduras	2.5	35.2	75.5	112.4	132.7	221.2
Nicaragua	6.2	33.7	108.5	124.5	131.1	0.0
Totals	26.9	253.4	484.6	484.6	584.0	1110.2

Source: Agency for International Development, Overseas Loans and Assistance from International Organizations, July 1945-September 1981, pp. 43, 47, 48, 51 and 54. Agency for International Development, Congressional Presentation, FY1984, Annex III, Latin America, (includes estimated expenditures), pp. 87, 138, 153, 201 and 221.

during the latter part of the decade. Violent student demonstrations awaited Vice President Richard M. Nixon's hemispheric tour in 1958. Fidel Castro's success in Cuba in 1959, not only deposed a staunch U.S. ally, Fulgencio Batista, but also demonstrated the emergence of the lower socioeconomic groups. Milton Eisenhower, the president's brother, also addressed the shortcomings of U.S. policy in his *The Wine Is Bitter*. These events contributed to President John F. Kennedy's 1961 warning that it was "one minute to midnight" in Latin America, and to his willingness to tolerate moderate leftist governments.

The Alliance for Progress, Peace Corps, and Food for Peace Program gave new hope to the region. During the next eight years U.S. economic assistance totaled $484.6 million (Table VII), nearly double the preceding eight. Housing construction, improved medical facilities, sanitation projects, improved farming techniques, and a literacy campaign reached many of the region's impoverished masses. By mid-decade, however, U.S. policy was dominated by the Vietnam war and domestic violence. Castro's isolation from the hemisphere and Lyndon Johnson's insistence on more friendly governments further lessened the concern with reform. The communist party was outlawed in each of the five Central American countries, and in 1964 the National Security Council concluded that the armed forces in each nation were capable of dealing with insurgency from clandestine groups. Given these considerations, President Johnson's 1968 visit to Central America was little more than window dressing.

The lack of concern with Central America continued under President Nixon. Between 1970 and 1974 economic assistance to the region was slashed by 50%. Only Nicaragua, because of the devastating earthquake in 1972, received any substantial help. Interest in the region was rekindled in 1974 when political crisis threatened its stability. Assistance appropriations for 1974 to 1976 brought the totals back to the Kennedy-Johnson levels, but it was too late. Central America was in the midst of violent turmoil.

In the thirty years following World War II, U.S. policy toward Central America sought to secure the region from communism. At first this meant incorporating the region into the defense network; but starting in the mid-1950s, the fear of internal subversion caused a redirection of policy to include programs to prepare the Central American military to deal with internal security. Early on, U.S. officials recognized that poverty served as a breeding ground for communism and they engaged in idealistic rhetoric calling for economic and social reform. Only at times when the region's tranquility

was threatened, however, did the United States invest in reform—
the Kennedy-Johnson years and from 1974 to 1976. One major
result of U.S. policy toward Central America was the entrenchment
of the elite, allied with the military. These groups resisted change.
The same conditions to which communism appealed in 1945 were
still there in 1976. The exception was Costa Rica, where the government was more representative of the people and sought to implement programs serving popular needs.

Crisis of the Old Order: Central America Today

Jimmy Carter arrived at the White House just as the current
Central American political turmoil began to erupt. At first, Carter
agreed with the report of the Center For Inter-American Relations
(commonly known as the Linowitz Report), which called for an end
to the outmoded policies of regionalism and paternalism. The new
policy was evident in the 1977 Panama Canal treaties. More important for Central America, however, was Carter's emphasis on human
rights as a prerequisite for a nation to receive economic and social
assistance from the United States. Human rights was not new to U.S.
foreign policy. Provisions in the 1973 Foreign Assistance Act, the
1975 Food Assistance Act, and the 1976 Security Assistance and
Arms Export Control Act provided for withholding aid where human
rights violations existed.

Carter promised a new emphasis on human rights, but found that
more than rhetoric was needed to persuade military-dominated
governments. He criticized the Central American dictators for their
human rights violations and in March 1977 halted military aid to
Guatemala and El Salvador for their actions. The withdrawal of aid,
however, had little impact on human rights. By 1980 violations increased by extremist groups, both left and right, and by the
Guatemalan and Salvadoran governments.

Carter's idealistic goals did not affect the realities of Central
American politics. These realities caused concern that history would
repeat itself and once again engulf the region in conflict. United
States security interests were threatened, and the cloak of communism appeared to hover over the region. Carter shifted his policy. The
administration sought to influence the political dynamics of the
region so that governments compatible with United States interests
would emerge.

Events in Nicaragua came first, where the Somoza dynasty, often threatened since 1945, now appeared to be crumbling under pressure from all segments of society. In 1977, the U.S. Department of State began to press Somoza for human rights reforms, in particular to lift the state of siege, which was done in September 1977. The assassination of *La Prensa* editor Pedro Joaquín Chamorro in January 1978 not only touched off a new round of violence in Nicaragua, but caused the United States to further separate itself from Somoza. The State Department cancelled a scheduled visit by Assistant Secretary of State for Inter-American affairs Terrance A. Todman, and because of its human rights violations, terminated Nicaragua's 1979 military assistance loan. In February 1978 the State Department announced that the U.S. supported efforts to achieve a democratic government in Nicaragua and denied any intention of military intervention on behalf of Somoza. The break seemed complete in June 1978 with the State Department declaration that it was opposed to the Somoza regime.

As often happened during Carter's administration, however, conflicting signals were sent out. In a secret letter to Somoza on June 30, 1978, Carter congratulated the dictator for inviting the Inter-American Commission on Human Rights to visit the country, for proposing amnesty for political prisoners, and for permitting the Committee of Twelve to return. When someone leaked the letter to the media in July, its congratulatory tone stunned Nicaraguan moderates. At the same time, the United States released to the Somoza government $12 million in economic aid budgeted for 1978. Both actions convinced the Broad Opposition Front (FAO) that the United States, despite its rhetoric, still supported the Somoza regime.

The National Guard's brutal suppression of the September 1978 insurrection brought new pressures upon Somoza to accept mediation. President Carter ordered U.S. naval cruisers to patrol near Nicaragua, and Congress deleted $8 million in economic assistance from the 1979 budget. Venezuela called for OAS mediation of the conflict to which Somoza agreed. An OAS mediation panel representing Guatemala, the United States and the Dominican Republic began its work in October. The rebel FAO issued a non-negotiable demand, rejected by Somoza, that the dictator immediately resign and leave the country with his family. The FSLN objected to any foreign mediation, especially to the U.S. proposal that an interim junta be formed to include National Guard representation. When negotiations broke down in mid-November, the FSLN renewed its military offensive. In the same month, the OAS Human Rights

Commission issued its report condemning Somoza's record. This report contributed to the U.S. veto of a $20 million International Monetary Fund loan to Nicaragua, and to its support of a United Nations General Assembly censure of Nicaragua for its human rights violations.

Somoza's harsh response to the increased fighting only increased his international isolation. By May 1979, prior to the "Final Offensive," Costa Rica and Mexico severed diplomatic relations; Brazil, Ecuador, Grenada, and Panama suspended relations; Britain recalled its ambassador; and the OAS Council called for Somoza's resignation. Both the U.S. Congress and administration decided to clearly abandon the dictator. In February, the United States its withdrew military attachés, Peace Corpsmen, and some diplomats from Nicaragua and suspended the remainder of appropriated, but yet undelivered, economic aid. In May all nonessential diplomatic personnel were brought home. The State Department publically expressed the opinion that only Somoza's resignation could end the fighting. International isolation further weakened Somoza's strength, already at a low ebb because of the broad based opposition and economic chaos at home.

Six days after the opposition's "Final Offensive" began on June 4, 1979, the Governing Junta of National Reconstruction was formed in San José, Costa Rica. It rejected Carter's appeal for an OAS multinational peacekeeping force for Nicaragua, and ignored his last proposal for a cease fire and an interim government to include the National Guard and PLN, but not the FSLN. When the United States finally conceded to FSLN representation on July 7, it was too late. All indicators pointed to an end of the Somoza dynasty and therefore there was no need for the FSLN to share power with any *Somocistas*, including interim President Francisco Urcuyo. On July 19, the Somoza dynasty ended and the following day, the FSLN-leaning junta inherited a country ravaged by war. From the start, the United States was unable to influence the FSLN administration.

The Sandinistas viewed the United States suspiciously because of its long history of intervention in the country, its collaboration with Somoza and Carter's efforts to keep the FSLN from power in 1978 and 1979. The Sandinistas were determined to pursue an independent foreign policy and were willing to treat the United States equal but not a privileged nation. Aid was welcomed from any country, and new markets with socialist and nonaligned countries anticipated. Under such circumstance diplomatic relations went fairly well until Carter left office. In the summer of 1979, the United States sent $8 million for reconstruction and Congress approved $30 million of a

$75 million direct loan. The United States did not militate against $241 million in loans from other sources—Agency for International Development, Inter-American Development Bank and World Bank. On the other hand, the Sandinista military buildup drew U.S. consternation, and Washingtion refused to supply arms unless accompanied by a U.S. training mission. The Sandinistas found military hardware and training elsewhere, including Panama, France, Cuba, and Eastern Bloc countries. The spurning of U.S. aid and conditions, coupled with the Sandinista restrictive domestic policy, contributed to a shift in U.S. attitude toward the end of Carter's administration.

Events within El Salvador also increased U.S. concern with Central American stability. The repression that previously caused Carter to halt military assistance, slash economic aid, and prevent an Inter-American Development Bank aid package, failed to stop the violence throughout the country. El Salvador appeared on the verge of civil war in 1979. Somoza's fall only increased the insecurity of the elite. Fearing for themselves, the military's younger officers staged a U.S. approved coup on October 15, 1979. The junta's effort to disband ORDEN, control inflation, and move towards land reform gave encouragement that "another Nicaragua" would be avoided. The United States supported the Salvadoran regime with $56 million for agrarian reform and other projects to aid the poor and with $5.6 million in military assistance to enable the Salvadoran Armed Forces to suppress violence, from both the left and the right. As Carter left office, however, the violence had not subsided.

With the Sandinista success in Nicaragua, the turmoil in El Salvador, and the continued violence in Guatemala, it appeared only natural that Honduras was next. Given this fear the United States encouraged Honduras on a path toward an elected president in 1980 by doubling its economic assistance to $59 million. The country's strategic importance did not go unnoticed and the United States provided $4 million in military assistance to tighten the Honduran borders against guerrilla activities and alleged Cuban arms shipments through Honduras to Salvadoran rebels. If Honduras became involved, could Costa Rica be far behind?

By 1980, a myriad of factors prevented the development of a clear U.S. policy toward Central America. The Carter administration appeared tolerant of leftist reform movements in Central America, a tolerance not shared by the region's elite or conservatives in the United States. On the other hand, rebel groups distrustful of the North Americans, wanted them out of Central America. Liberal groups in the United States pressed for stronger action against human rights violations. Under these varied pressures, Carter left the presidency without taking definitive action.

Ronald Reagan's election in 1980 caused yet another shift in U.S. policy toward Central America. The new administration was convinced that U.S. power and prestige had dwindled in the preceding four years in the face of Soviet-Cuban expansion and was convinced of the need to save Central America from communist incursions. Reagan's determination came from two sources: (1) the belief that Carter had been too tolerant of leftist regimes which permitted communist influence to spread; and (2) the convictions of the Defense Department and the intelligence community that U.S. supremacy should be reasserted in the Caribbean. Also Central America was the most plausible area in which to respond forcefully to Soviet-Cuban advances. Failure to act close to home, in the administration's view, only would encourage the Soviets to seek advances elsewhere.

Reagan's first foreign policy team, which included Secretary of State Alexander Haig, Assistant Secretary of State for Latin American Affairs Thomas O. Enders, and U.N. Ambassador Jeane Kirkpatrick reflected this view. New ambassadors, Dean Hinton to El Salvador and John Negroponte to Honduras also were considered "hard liners." By the time George Schultz replaced Haig and Langhorne H. Motley succeeded Enders, the new policy was entrenched. The administration became more tolerant of repressive governments, bringing criticism from liberals in both the United States and Central America. Reagan also emphasized a military solution, including increased military aid to Salvador, support for Nicaraguan *contras*, lifting the arms embargo against Guatemala, and conducting "war games" in Honduras. The increased U.S. emphasis on military activity stimulated a wide-spread fear that war would engulf the entire region. Finally, Reagan's proposed economic assistance, including the Caribbean Basin Initiative, was designed to help correct the long standing socioeconomic inequities that had plagued Central American society.

The Reagan administration shared Carter's view that a leftist victory in El Salvador had to be prevented. The failure in January 1981 of the guerrilla offensive presented the possibility of a negotiated settlement. Reagan, however, rejected the suggestion because it would have given the leftists an entry into government and, in so doing, encourage leftists elsewhere in the region. Thus, the United States continued to support Napoleon Duarte's government and its plans for agrarian and constitutional reform, while seeking a military solution.

In March 1981, the State Department issued a "White Paper," documenting alleged Cuban-Soviet support of the Salvadoran guerrillas. Based upon captured documents, the State Department claimed that some 200 tons of military supplies were shipped to the guerrillas through Cuba and Nicaragua. Castro also was accused of bringing together the diverse Salvadoran guerrilla factions into a united front, which resulted in the January 1981 offensive. In short, the State Department concluded that the insurgency in El Salvador had been transformed into a textbook case of indirect armed aggression by communist powers operating through Cuba.

Subsequently some observers criticized the "White Paper" for its vagueness and lack of substantial proof, but its immediate impact favored Reagan. He was able to increase U.S. military and economic assistance to the Duarte government. The United States advanced an additional $25 million for security assistance, increased the number of U.S. training personnel from 19 to 45, and allotted an additional $63 million in economic assistance for the 1981 fiscal year. Duarte responded with the appointment of an Electoral Commission to prepare the country for election of a Constitutional Assembly in March 1982.

For the next year Salvadoran troops trained in the United States and Panama and received improved weaponry. The government carried out Phase I of the government's land reform program. Military victory, however, was not in sight. Privately, U.S. military officials doubted that the Salvadoran army could turn the tide as evidence mounted that much of the new military equipment was falling into guerrilla hands. The guerrillas claimed control over an estimated 70,000 to 100,000 of the population. As terrorism from both the left and the right continued, the government appeared to be hedging on its pledge to find those responsible for the 1980 killing of the four U.S. churchwomen. The situation contributed to fears in the U.S. of another Vietnam. Congress expressed this concern in 1981 when it called for the administration to certify progress in human rights field every six months as a condition for continued assistance to the Salvadoran government. The March 1982 elections, although not disrupted by the abstaining guerrillas, did not go well for the United States. The rightist parties won control of the assembly over Duarte's centrist group.

In the twenty months that followed the election of Provisional President Alvaro Alfredo Magaña, the situation in El Salvador appeared to worsen. The FMLN's October 1982 offensive resulted in the capture of major cities in Morozan and Chalatenango provinces. The four day seizure of Berlin in Usulutan province in January 1983 had greater impact. Berlin was the largest city ever held by the guerrillas, causing doubt about the effectiveness of government troops. In driving the rebels from Berlin, indiscriminate air strikes with U.S.

supplied aircraft raised further questions about the government's ability to win over the people, as well as extent of United States involvement. Reagan continued to insist on a military solution, while rejecting peace overtures from Mexico and France following the Berlin seizure by the FMLN-FDR forces.

In March 1983, Reagan convinced the Salvadoran military to initiate civic action programs in an effort to win support from the rural population. The release of a second "White Paper" in May 1983 more clearly established the Cuban-Nicaraguan link to the Salvadoran rebels. By fall 1983 the FMLN forces claimed control over most of Chalatenango and Morozan provinces, and portions of La Union and Usulutan provinces. Journalists reported popular support for the guerrillas in these largely rural and lightly inhabited regions. Human rights violations remained a significant problem for Reagan, who faced stiff congressional opposition in the recertification process in January and July 1983. By using the "pocket veto" in November 1983, the president ignored congressional concern for human rights. The reassignment, under U.S. pressure, of Salvadoran military officers associated with the right wing death squads did little to assuage liberal criticism in the United States. The situation in Salvador by year's end appeared, at best, to be a stalemate.

The Salvadoran crisis also became part of Reagan's larger regional policy that centered on Nicaragua. Mutual distrust between Reagan and the Marxist orientated Sandinistas made a conflict between the United States and Nicaragua almost inevitable. Documentation from State Department and intelligence sources that Nicaragua was supplying arms to the Salvadoran rebels convinced Reagan of a communist menace to Central America. The FSLN's restrictions on speech and press freedoms and prevention of labor union organizations violated congressional requirements for the lifting of economic assistance and contributed to Reagan's perception of it being a dictatorial regime. Government expansion into the economic sector, at the expense of the private sector, increased trade contacts with communist bloc countries and the presence of foreign, particularly Cuban, advisors, reaffirmed the administration's judgement that Central America fell under the umbrella of the east-west confrontation.

Shortly after his inauguration, President Reagan approved CIA covert support for the Nicaraguan *contras.* Some 150 CIA agents were reportedly training and supplying these Honduran-based forces. Following the admission of such support, Reagan continued to request and receive from congress funds to continue the *contras* operations. The intention of the U.S. backed operation, according to CIA Director William Casey was threefold: (1) to retaliate for Nicaraguan help to the Salvadoran guerrillas; (2) to interdict Nicaraguan arms shipments to the guerrillas; and (3) to pressure the FSLN to negotiate with its internal opposition and with the United States to ease regional tensions. Congressional liberals—such as Tom Harkin, Edward Boland, Michael Barnes, Christopher Dodd and Paul Tsongas—challenged the administration's claim that it did not intend to overthrow the Sandinistas. On the other hand conservatives like Chairman Jesse Helms of the Senate's Western Hemisphere Affairs Subcommittee, supported the president's efforts to stop the spread of communism. Aid to the estimated 2000 *contras* continued. Their success was limited to destruction of bridges, crop burning and, in November 1983, blowing up oil storage tanks, by far their most notable achievement.

The *contra's*, however, were not able to take the war to the cities, capture a sizeable chunk of territory, or establish a provisional government. Reportedly, Casey has consistently told congressional intelligence panels that the *contras* were not strong enough to topple the Sandinistas. The Pentagon's Defense Intelligence Agency concluded in July 1982 that the rebels posed no serious threat to the Nicaraguan government. Critics paralleled aid to the *contras* with that supplied to anti-Castro forces in 1960-61. As the Cuban rebels were largely pro-Batista, the *contras* were *Somocistas*, who represented the old regime and unlikely to gain popular support. Under congressional pressure, the CIA in late 1983 reportedly pressured the *contras* into making significant progress by February 1, 1984, or face a cutoff of funds.

Military pressure was not the only avenue pursued by the Reagan administration against Nicaragua. Immediately on entering the White House, the president cancelled $9.6 million in credits for the purchase of Nicaraugan wheat, $15 million in economic aid and $11 million in rural development, health and education loans. The United States also blocked Inter-American Development Bank and World Bank loans and attempted to dissuade private U.S. banks from participating in international loan agreements with Nicaragua. The effort to disrupt commercial relations has been less effective. In May 1983, the United States cut the Nicaraguan sugar quota by 90%, but the Sandinistas found new markets in Iran, Algeria and the Soviet Union. Despite a pullout of the Standard Fruit Company, bananas from Nicaragua still have made their way to the west coast of the United States. The total impact of U.S. economic policy has disrupted in the Nicaraguan economy, but not caused its collapse.

Honduras did not escape the drift of events. Transition to civilian rule in November 1981, with the presidential election of Roberto Suazo Córdoba, and the subsequent $150 million in United States economic assistance had little impact on the region's poorest country. Many observers believed that the armed forces, staunchly anti-communist, remained the real political power, and that it would act if Honduran stability were threatened.

Honduras was in a precarious position. As host to the CIA-supported *contras*, it was constantly threatened with retaliation by Nicaragua. Its Salvadoran and Guatemalan border areas were considered havens for rebels operating in those countries, a fact which contributed to the fear of intervention. Guerrilla groups also operated within the country. The most notable was the Cinchonero Popular Liberation Movement (Cinchoneros), considered by Honduran authorities to be an arm of the Salvadoran FMLN. By late 1982, the Cinchoneros in Honduras were credited with over $2 million in ransoms and robberies. The group's most publicized episode occurred in September 1982 when it seized the Chamber of Commerce Building in San Pedro Sula and held more than 100 hostages. Their demand for release of an estimated 80 political prisoners failed, but the government granted the twelve leftists who seized the building with safe conduct out of the country.

The United States has placed heavy importance on Honduras. By the summer of 1983, some $253 million in economic aid had been dispersed, the Agency for International Development supported the sale of Honduran bonds to help close its foreign debt, and 247 Peace Corps volunteers were in Honduras. The embassy in Tegulcigalpa had a full time diplomatic staff of 110, and an estimated 300 military advisors were in the country. The military presence increased throughout 1983 and 1984 with support personnel used in Honduran troop training exercises along the Nicaraguan border in February, with the establishment of a Green Beret camp at Trujillo, and with the five thousand U.S. troops used in the Big Pine exercises during the fall. The military operations may have been designed to intimidate the Sandinistas, but they did not. Rather, the Nicaraguan government used the incidents to inflame popular emotion against the United States and to prepare for a possible U.S. invasion.

Guatemala and Costa Rica received new considerations. In August 1983, two days prior to the overthrow of Ríos Montt in Guatemala, General Mejía Victores met on the U.S. aircraft carrier *Ranger* with high ranking Honduran, Salvadoran and U.S. military officials. Mejía Victores' subsequent declaration in support of Reagan's Central American policies gave credence to the argument that the U.S. had approved the coup that ousted Montt. By year's end Reagan moved toward lifting the arms embargo imposed on Guatemala, but the outcry against increased human rights violations restrained him. Traditionally neutral Costa Rica received increased military and technical assistance during Reagan's first three years in office and, as anti-Nicaraguan rebels increased their base of operations in Costa Rica, the speculation increased that Costa Rica would be drawn into the region's conflict.

Four other Reagan efforts demonstrated his policy directions. Two initiatives were diplomatic, one economic, and one military. The latter had the greatest impact. First, former democratic Senator Richard Stone was appointed special envoy to the region in June 1983. The hope was that Stone could bring together the various Central American factions to agree on peace plan for the entire region. This included working with the so-called Contadora Group—Mexico, Panama, Colombia, and Venezuela—which proposed that Latin American nations pursue their own solution to regional problems. The Contadora peace plan called for withdrawal of all foreign military personnel, disarmament and regional negotiations. No sooner had Stone returned from his two week initial fact finding mission, than Reagan took his second diplomatic initiative. Henry Kissinger was appointed chairman of a high level bi-partisan commission to recommend long term policy toward the region. Following testimony from economic, military, and political leaders, including former presidents Nixon, Ford, and Carter, the commission toured Central America. If Stone's appointment was designed to blunt the rising domestic criticism against Reagan's current military policy, Kissinger's appointment was designed to quiet those demanding a long term policy.

The economic initiative was found in the Caribbean Basin Initiative, proposed by Reagan in February 1982 and finally passed by Congress at the end of its 1983 session. Excluding Nicaragua, the CBI seeks to encourage industrial development through private investment, trade through tariff relief from the United States, and development through U.S. financial assistance. While recipient governments anticipate economic development, critics in the U.S. claim that political instability will thwart private investment.

Finally in October 1983, Reagan ordered 5000 U.S. troops to invade the island of Grenada, ostensibly to rescue 700 U.S. medical students at St. George. Of greater importance may have been the airport being constructed by Cuban technicians and designed to handle large jet aircraft. From available evidence, the U.S. landing force met resistance from Cuban soldiers, disguised as construction workers, and discovered Cuban and Soviet arms caches, and Communist Bloc military advisers. The latter discoveries received greater publicity than Reagan's "gunboat diplomacy." The invasion's impact was not lost on Managua which, after whipping up invasion hysteria, directed the removal of some Cuban military personnel, announced plans to halt arms supplies to the Salvadoran guerrillas, and issued "feelers" hinting at possible acceptance of a diplomatic solution to the regional crisis.

Stone resigned his post about the about the same time the Kissinger commission report appeared in January 1984. Each caused new controversey over the direction of President Reagan's policy. Stone reportedly resigned because of personal differences with Assistant Secretary of State for Latin American Affairs, Langorne Motley. Stone's replacement, Harry Shlaudeman, served in Chile during the covert operations under the Nixon administration that deposed Marxist President Salvadore Allende. This association caused congressional protest.

More significant was the Kissinger report which recognized the strategic importance of the region to the United States. "Central America's crisis is our crisis," the report concluded. Therefore, the commission emphasized the U.S. goal of preventing the establisment of a Soviet foothold in Central America either directly, or through Cuba. To achieve that goal the commission recommended increased military aid to the region, but also recognizing the underlying socio-economic causes of the crisis, the commission recommended an $8 billion array of economic development and social reform packages. Reagan's supporters applauded the report. Communist expansion would be stopped, to be followed by economic and social assistance. The United States would assume responsibility for ending the crisis. Critics deplored the military recommendations, which they charged would deepen the crisis and vastly increase U.S. involvement. Instead the critics called for increased economic assistance and a negotiated settlement that included Cuba.

Spurred by the Kissinger report, Congress approved increased economic assistance for Central America before recessing in October 1984. The economic assistance was overshadowed by new revelations of CIA assistance to the *contras* for the purpose of overthrowing the Sandinista regime, not for the interdiction of arms supplies to the Salvadoran rebels.

In April 1984, the CIA was found to have supervised the mining of three Nicaraguan ports—Corinto, Puerto Sandino and El Bluff. Reportedly, twelve merchant ships from six countries, including the Soviet Union, were damaged by the crudely made mines. At least fifteen crewmen were injured in these incidents. Nicaragua took the issue to the World Court, which found the United States guilty and instructed the removal of the mines. Before the Court's decision was rendered, however, the Reagan administration announced that it would ignore the Court's Central American rulings for two years. Congressional opposition to funding for the *contras* was further stiffened by the revelation that the CIA failed to inform the Senate Select Committee on Intelligence about the mining of Nicaragua's harbors and, in October 1984, the committee learned of a CIA manual that instructed the *contras* in political terrorism, including assassination.

The Reagan administration also ignored the Contadora process. In late August 1984, the Contadora group completed a fifty-one page draft treaty. Its major provisions called for mutual reductions in arms and troops; a limitation on and ultimate elimination of foreign military advisors; a prohibition of foreign military bases in Central America and support for guerrilla forces seeking to overthrow governments in the region. The United States found the proposal flawed and anticipated that Nicaragua would balk at the provisions against the introduction of new weapons, assistance to guerrilla groups and free elections. The Sandinistas, however, announced that they would sign the draft treaty and challenged the United States and its Central American allies to do the same. When the governments of Costa Rica, El Salvador, Guatemala and Honduras subsequently expressed favor with the draft treaty, the United States was the embarrassed lone dissenter.

Taken together, these events contributed to the congressional refusal in October 1984 to approve an additional $21 million in aid for the *contras*, and a warning to the CIA not to use its contingency fund to assist the Nicaraguan rebel groups.

The opposition within the United States had an impact upon its Central American allies. The *contras*, and the Honduran and Salvadoran military protested U.S. interference in their training and procedures. The *contras* also admitted that the interdiction of arm supplies to the Salvadoran rebels was not their top priority, which was the overthrow the Sandinistas. The Guatemalan government claimed that it could live with the Sandinistas. On election eve, the Reagan administration found opposition to its Central American policy both at home and abroad.

President Reagan's resounding re-election victory in November 1984 failed to provide him with a clear mandate on Central American policy. The Republican Party failed to gain control of congress; nor was the president presented with an ideological working majority.

Reagan's response to the alleged Soviet effort to ship MIG-21 fighter planes to Nicaragua, however, indicated that he would continue to pursue a military solution to the Central American crisis. Although the aircraft were not a threat to United States security, they were to the *contras.* If delivered, Reagan promised their destruction either with a surgical airstrike or *contra* directed sabotage. Reportedly, Reagan also considered a quarantine of all military supplies to the Nicaraguan government. The prospects for a peaceful solution appear remote.

Summary

Since the independence of Central America in 1823, U.S. policy toward the region has been dominated by the determination to keep Europeans out and to ensure the security of U.S. interests. During the nineteenth century the British were the primary concern; in the twentieth century, prior to World War II, concern focused on European commercial expansion; while after World War II, the United States perceived international communism to be a threat to its security. Throughout, the United States sought political and financial stability in the region and often employed military means to achieve it. In so doing the United States sided with the established elite and ignored the demands of the middle and lower sectors in Central America.

III

Conclusion

Central America's historical development and U.S. policy toward the region are bonded by the fact that each contributed to the contemporary crisis, but for different reasons. Regional leaders deliberately sought to maintain their political and economic privileges and social status. The United States always sought to keep foreigners out, and in the twentieth century supported political stability in an effort to achieve regional security. In pursuing their separate objectives, both Central American leaders and United States policymakers failed to incorporate the middle and lower sectors into the region's mainstream.

The history of each Central American nation varies, notably Costa Rica, where the military's presence was less marked, and the transfer of political power was generally peaceful. The governments of all five nations, however, were dominated by the elite landowners. This aristocratic system developed from Spanish colonial policy and continued following independence in 1823. Consequently, the liberal-conservative struggle for power in the early nineteenth century was a contest limited to the landowners in each country.

Liberal policies after 1871 not only widened the gap between rich and poor, but also contributed to the development of an articulate middle sector. In their quest for material progress the positivist liberals permitted foreign capital, largely North American, to develop the banana industry and accompanying infrastructure and commercial pursuits. This economic advancement contributed to the growing political strength of the middle sector which by the 1920s pressed for entry into the political process. At the same time, labor leaders demanded improved living standards for the lower socioeconomic groups. The elite, using the military (except in Costa Rica), resisted change, and labeled such demands as communistic. The dictators that emerged in the 1930s reflected the elite's views and forcefully suppressed opposition to the status quo.

Middle sector pressure resulted in some gains immediately following World War II, but after 1949 the pattern of repressive governments returned. The elite expanded their control over local economies, further widening the standard of living between rich and poor. Middle sector organizations demanding political change, labor groups seeking improved living standards, and guerrilla brigades in the countryside were again labeled communists and suppressed by the military. The elite sought to maintain the established order.

Costa Rica, again, was an exception to this pattern. A civil war in 1949 dislodged the elite. Thereafter, the government was more democratic, and it also implemented economic and social reform programs. The military, never a major political factor, was disbanded. By 1977 Costa Rica's living standard stood above those of its neighbors, but the benefits did not reach all Costa Ricans.

Two events in 1972 triggered the immediate causes of Central America's contemporary crisis. A devasting earthquake in Managua, Nicaragua, led to the coalescence of all groups opposing Somoza. His brutal suppression of the opposition groups only increased their determination to force his ouster which came in July 1979. In El Salvador, in 1972, Christian Democrat José Napolean Duarte won the presidential election, but was denied office by the military. The military's ruthless suppression of opposition groups that followed failed to head off the civil war that erupted in 1980, and threatened to engulf the entire region. This threat also brought in the United States.

Nineteenth-century efforts by the United States to deal with foreign interlopers in Central America began with Great Britain, whose regional expansionary plans were limited by the 1850 Clayton-Bulwer Treaty. U.S. interest in the region waned except for a brief period in the 1870's when the French sought unsuccessfully to build a transisthmian canal.

In the twentieth century, construction of the Panama Canal brought Central America under the U. S. security umbrella. While its policies continued to discourage European interests, the United States also sought to encourage political stability in the region. The period 1907 to 1933 was marked by U.S. attempts to impose constitutionalism and fiscal responsibility on Central American governments and, at the same time, to end the dominant political role of the military. These efforts failed, but did contribute to the Good Neighbor Policy, which permitted toleration of the dictatorships that emerged in the 1930's. Whether intervention or nonintervention, however, U.S. policies had the same effect: the elite remained entrenched in power, the military's political role was enhanced, the demands and needs of the middle and lower sectors were unattended, and U. S. private investments were secured.

After World War II, Central America became a microcosm of U.S. Cold War responses to communism. Except for the years 1961 to 1963, U.S. policy emphasized a military solution to the region's problems. The Truman administration perceived no direct communist threat to Central America and, therefore, was content with its incorporation into the United Nations and Organization of American States. In 1954 Secretary of State John Foster Dulles incorrectly linked Guatemalan leftist reformers to Moscow as justification for U.S. support of the overthrow of the Arbenz regime. Thereafter presidential reasons differed, but U.S. military aid programs to Central America increased. Significantly, the aid strengthened the local military in its battle against alleged communists, and further cemented its relationship with the landowning elite which further diminished the prospects for democratic government. The Alliance for Progress, although a response to Castro's revolution in Cuba, suggested that Washington achieved an understanding of middle and lower sector ambitions, but the program fell victim to U.S. involvement in Vietnam. Historically, the United States dealt with Central America's elite and, consequently, its policies served to entrench the elite's privileged positions.

When confronted with the crisis that erupted in 1977, President Jimmy Carter's human rights policy did not deal with the underlying socioeconomic issues. The cutoff of U. S. military aid did not deter human rights violations, but did contribute to the fall of the Somoza dynasty in 1979. Carter's confused policy toward the Sandinistas in Nicaragua and rebels in Salvador is understandable within the historical framework of U.S. policy toward Central America: the old order was crumbling, and the emerging revolutionary forces were not understood.

So too, is Reagan's proposed military solution. As the "gunboat diplomacy" in the early 1900s, intervention in the 1920s, and military aid after World War II sought to secure the region from foreign interlopers, increased military activities in the 1980's are designed to keep "communism" out. Such solutions, however, continue to ignore middle and lower sector aspirations.

The record of Central American history and United States policy toward the region clearly indicate that the Marxist-oriented revolutionaries and tradition-bound U. S. policymakers are incompatible, and that understanding between the two is most unlikely. Two extreme options are available to the United States: (1) total withdrawal from the region, and (2) imposition of a military solution. A third alternative, recommended by the Contadora group, appears more plausible: recognition that the forces of change make the status of the old order untenable, and that working for constructive change is more promising than resisting it. Debate over these policy options will occupy the foreseeable future.

IV

Selected Bibliography

The materials cited below have been divided into four general categories: (1) Central American History, (2) United States—Central American Relations, (3) The Contemporary Crisis, and (4) Reference Works. In the first three sections there has been a deliberate effort to identify materials in English largely because of their availability and because of the intended audience of this book. Also the materials cited in the first two sections often overlap. The third section brings together materials dealing with the years since 1976, a time period in which it is nearly impossible to separate citations that deal solely with either the region's domestic crisis or United States policy. The final section, Reference Works, includes many Spanish language sources, since English-language materials are often scarce for the Central American countries.

Central American History

HISTORICAL SURVEYS

The most recent historical survey of the region is Ralph Lee Woodward's *Central America: A Nation Divided* [entry 18]. It is an interpretative analysis focusing upon the liberal-conservative struggle that developed in the nineteenth century. Three other standard works, emphasizing political developments include Willian H. Koebel [entry 6], Mario Rodríguez [entry 11], and Franklin D. Parker [entry 10]. Richard N. Adams, *Cultural Survey* [entry 2] is valuable for its study of society. Earlier studies are important for their descriptive contributions. Notable are the works of United States Minister to Central America, E. George Squier [entries 14, and 15] and British traveler, Carl Scherzer [entry 13].

An excellent political analysis is Thomas P. Anderson's *Politics in Central America* [entry 4]. The middle sector struggle against the dictatorships immediately following World War II is covered by Charles Ameringer and Thomas M. Leonard [entries 3 and 7].

The impact of the Spanish colonial system upon the region is found in Murdo J. MacLeod's *Spanish Central America* [entry 8]. Of related importance is the question of Central American political and economic union, see entries 35 through 56.

1 Adams, Frederick Upham. *Conquest of the Tropics.* Garden City, N.Y.: Doubleday, 1914.

2 Adams, Richard N. *Cultural Survey of Panama, Nicaragua, Guatemala, El Salvador, Honduras.* Washington, D.C.: Pan American Sanitary Bureau, 1957.

3 Ameringer, Charles. *The Democratic Left in Exile: The Antidictatorial Struggle in the Caribbean, 1945-1959.* Coral Gables, Fla.: University of Miami Press, 1974.

4 Anderson, Thomas P. *Politics in Central America.* New York: Praeger, 1982.

5 Bancroft, Hubert Howe. *History of Central America.* 3 vols. San Francisco: The History Company 1883-1887.

6 Koebel, William H. *Central America: Guatemala, Nicaragua, Costa Rica, Honduras, Panama, and Salvador.* London: Fisher Unwin, 1925.

7 Leonard, Thomas M. *United States and Central America, 1944-1949: Perceptions of Political Dynamics.* University: University of Alabama Press, 1984.

8 MacLeod, Murdo J. *Spanish Central America: A Socioeconomic History.* Berkeley: University of California Press, 1973.

9 Needler, Martin C., ed. *Political Systems of Latin America.* Princeton, N.J.: Princeton University Press, 1964.

10 Parker, Franklin D. *The Central American Republics.* London: Oxford University Press, 1964.

11 Rodríguez, Mario. *Central America.* Englewood Cliffs, N.J.: Prentice-Hall, 1965.

12 Sanders, William T., and Barbara J. Price. *Mesoamerica: The Evolution of a Civilization.* New York: Random House, 1968.

13 Scherzer, Carl. *Travels in the Free States of Central America: Nicaragua, Honduras, and San Salvador.* London: Longman, Brown, Green, Longmans, and Roberts, 1857.

14 Squier, E. George. *Notes on Central America.* New York: Harper, 1855.

15 _____. *The Serpent Symbol, and the Worship of the Reciprocal Principles of Nature in America.* New York: Putman, 1851.

16 Wilgus, A. Curtis, ed. *The Caribbean: The Central American Area.* Gainesville: University of Florida Press, 1961.

17 Wilson, Charles Morrow. *Central American Challenge and Opportunity.* New York: Holt, 1941.

18 Woodward, Ralph Lee. *Central America, A Nation Divided.* New York: Oxford University Press, 1976 [rev. ed. 1985].

CONTEMPORARY CONFLICT

The current crisis is traced to the fall of Nicaraguan strongman Anastasio Somoza in July 1979. Three brief analysis of the crisis are found in the Richard E. Feinberg and Richard Millett essays [entries 22, 23 and 30]. Revisionist approaches include "Central America: The Strongmen are Shaking" and Walter LaFeber's *Inevitable Revolutions* [entries 20 and 26]. An excellent collection of essays, covering several dimensions of the crisis, is *Central America: Anatomy of Conflict* [entry 27].

Because the contemporary conflict cannot be separated from U.S. foreign policy, see "Contemporary Conflict" [entries 365 through 387] and "Policy Recommendations" [entries 396 through 402].

19 Bushnell, John A. "Central America." *Current* 250 (Feb. 1983), 37-42.

20 "Central America: The Strongmen are Shaking." *Latin American Perspectives* 25 and 26 (Spring/Summer 1980), 2-189.

21 Ebel, Ronald H. "Political Instability in Central America," *Current History* 81 (Feb. 1982), 49-51+.

22 Feinberg, Richard E. "Central America: No Easy Answers" *Foreign Affairs* 59 (Summer 1981), 1121-59.

23 _____, ed. *Central America: International Dimensions of the Crisis.* New York: Holmes & Meier, 1982.

24 Grabendorf, Wolf and Heinrich Krumwiede, eds. *Political Change in Central America: Internal and External Dimensions.* Boulder, CO: Westview, 1984.

25 Griffin, Keith B. *Land Concentration and Rural Poverty.* New York: Holmes & Meier, 1976.

26 LaFeber, Walter. *Inevitable Revolutions: The United States in Central America.* New York: Norton, 1983.

27 Leiken, Robert S., ed. *Central America: Anatomy of Conflict.* New York: Pergamon, 1984.

28 "Military Excesses and Democratic Hypes." *Center Magazine* 15 (Jan./ Feb. 1982), 37-59.

29 Millett, Richard. "Central American Cauldron." *Current History* 82 (Feb. 1983), 69-73 ff.

30 _____. "Central American Paralysis." *Foreign Policy* 39 (Summer 1980), 99-117.

31 Riding, Alan. "The Central American Quagmire." *Foreign Affairs* 61 (Special Issue, 1982), 641-59.

32 Schulz, Donald E. and Douglas H. Graham, eds. *Revolution in Central America and the Caribbean.* Boulder, CO: Westview, 1984.

33 Stanford Central American Action Network, ed. *Revolution in Central America.* Boulder, CO: Westview, 1983.

34 "Struggle in Central America." [a symposium] *Foreign Policy* 43 (Summer 1981), 70-103.

INTEGRATION AND UNION

The question of union is one of the overriding themes in the study of Central America. Thomas L. Karnes *The Failure of Union* [entry 45] is the most significant work on the subject. Like John Martz's biography of Justino Barrios [entry 47], it emphasizes the political aspects of integration. The establishment of the Central American Common Market in 1960 brought forth a number of economic studies. James D. Cochrane's *Politics of Regional Integration* [entry 39] and Carlos Castillo's *Growth and Integration* [entry 38] are good starting points. Excellent analysis of the market can be found in

Stuart Fagan [entry 41] and Gary Wynia [entry 56]. Both demonstrate how the region's political rivalries influenced the market's development.

35 Bachmura, Frank T. "Toward Economic Reconcilation in Central America." *World Affairs* 133 (Mar. 1971), 283-292.

36 Bishop, Jefferson M. *Arévalo and Central American Unification.* Baton Rouge: Lousiana State University Press, 1971.

37 Cable, Vinceno. "The 'Football War' and The Central American Common Market." *International Affairs* 45 (Oct. 1969), 658-671.

38 Castillo, Carlos. *Growth and Integration in Central America.* New York: Praeger, 1966.

39 Cochrane, James D. *The Politics of Regional Intergration: The Central American Case.* New Orleans: Tulane University Press, 1969.

40 _____. "U. S. Attitudes Towards Central American Intergration." *Inter-American Economic Affairs* 18 (1964), 1971.

41 Fagan, Stuart I. *Central American Economic Integration: The Politics of Unequal Benefits.* Los Angeles: University of California International Studies, 1970.

42 Grieb, Kenneth J. "The United States and the Central American Federation." *The Americas* 24 (Oct. 1967), 107-121.

43 Grunewald, Joseph, Miguel S. Wionczek; and Martin C. Martin. *Latin American Economic Integration and U. S. Policy.* Washington, D.C.: Brookings Institution, 1972.

44 Hansen, Robert. *Central America: Regional Integration and Economic Development.* Washington, D.C.: National Planning Association, 1967.

45 Karnes, Thomas L. *The Failure of Union: Central America, 1824-1975.* Tempe: Arizona State University Press, 1976.

46 Landry, David M. "U. S. Policy and Lessons Learned from the Central American Economic Integration Experience." *Southern Quarterly* 11 (1973), 297-308.

47 Martz, John D. *Justo Rufino Barrios and Central American Union.* Gainesville: University of Florida Press, Latin American Monographs, No. 21, 1962.

48 May, Charles P. *Central America: Lands Seeking Unity.* Toronto: Thomas Nelson, 1966.

49 McClelland, Donald H. *The Central American Common Market: Economic Policies, Economic Growth and Choices for the Future.* New York: Praeger, 1972.

50 Nye, Joseph A. *Central American Integration.* New York: Appleton-Century Crofts, 1967.

51 Orantes, Isaac C. *Regional Integration in Central America.* Lexington, MA: D.C. Heath, 1973.

52 Ramsett, David E. *Regional Industrial Development in Central America: A Case Study of the Integration Industries Scheme.* New York: Praeger, 1969.

53 Schmitter, Philippe C. *Autonomy or Dependence as Regional Integration Outcomes: Central America.* Berkeley: Institute of International Studies, University of California, 1972.

54 Slade, William F. "Federation of Central America." *Journal of Race Development* 8 (Oct. 1917), 234-241.

55 Smith, Robert S. "Financing the Central American Federation, 1821-1838." *Hispanic American Historical Review* 43 (Nov. 1963), 483-510.

56 Wynia, Gary W. *Politics and Planners: Economic Development in Central America.* Madision: University of Wisconsin Press, 1972.

LIBERATION THEOLOGY

The Catholic Church has become embroiled in the contemporary Central American crisis. Clerical proponents of social change, even through revolution, adhere to liberation theology. Excellent overviews of the topic are found in *Doing Theology in a Revolutionary Situation* and *Theology in a New Key* [entries 59 and 63]. Both, also have extensive bibliographies. Gustavo Guieterrez's *A Theology of Liberation* [entry 60] is considered to be one of the best analysis of the theology's social impact. C. Peter Wagner [entry 65] criticizes liberation theology from an evangelical perspective. The Church's activist political role is traced to the 1968 Bishop's conference at Medallín, Colombia. The conference documents [entry 61] are important for understanding the Church's work on behalf of the poor.

57 Assman, Hugo. *Theology for a Nomad Church.* Maryknoll, N.Y.: ORBIS, 1976.

58 Brockman, J. R. "The Prophetic Role of the Church in Latin America." *Christian Century* 100 (Oct. 19, 1983), 931-935.

59 Brown, Robert M. *Theology in a New Key.* Philadelphia: Westminster Press, 1968.

60 Gutiérrez, Gustavo. *A Theology of Liberation.* Maryknoll, N.Y.: ORBIS, 1971.

61 Latin American Episcopal Council (CELAM). *The Church in the Present Day Transformation of Latin America in the Light of The Council.* Bogotá: General Secretariat of CELAM, 1970.

62 McGovern, A. F. "Liberation Theology in Actual Progress." *Commonweal* 110 (Jan. 28, 1983), 46-49.

63 Miguez-Bonino, José. *Doing Theology in a Revolutionary Situation.* Philadelphia: Fortress Press, 1973.

64 "Polarization in the Church." *Commonweal* 111 (May 18, 1984), 291-293.

65 Wagner, C. Peter. *Latin American Theology: Radical or Evangelical?.* Grand Rapids, Mich.: Wm. B. Eerdmans, 1970.

National Histories

For those unfamiliar with the five Central American countries, a good beginning is the *Country Studies* series [entries 68, 93, 134, 198 and 228]. Each provides a brief historical summary, description of the economy and social structure, and an analysis of the political institutions, the military and the Church.

COSTA RICA

Adequate surveys of Costa Rica include John and Mavis Biesanz, *Costa Rican Life* [entry 66], Charles Denton *Patterns of Costa Rican Politics* [entry 69], and Chester Lloyd Jones *Costa Rica and Civilization in the Caribbean* [entry 71]. Costa Rica often avoided regional turmoil, which is the focus of two important studies by Richard Salisbury [entries 88 and 89]. Both illustrate the nation's attitude towards its neighbors in the 1920s. The 1948 Civil War is the most highlighted topic of twentieth century Costa Rican history. John Bell's *Crisis in Costa Rica* [entry 79] provides an excellent analysis, illustrating the use of the communist issue by upper class groups.

Charles Ameringer's sympathetic biography of José Figueres [entry 78] and Burt L. English's *Liberación Nacional* [entry 81] provide excellent analysis of the middle sector.

General

66 Biesanz, John and Mavis Biesanz. *Costa Rican Life.* New York: Columbia University Press, 1944.

67 Blanco Segura, Ricardo. *Historia eclesiástica de Costa Rica.* San José, Costa Rica: 1967.

68 Blutstein, Howard I., et al. *Area Handbook: Costa Rica.* Washington, D.C.: G.P.O., 1970.

69 Denton, Charles F. *Patterns of Costa Rican Politics.* Boston: Allyn & Bacon, 1971.

70 Goldrich, Daniel. *Sons of the Establishment: Elite Youth in Panama and Costa Rica.* Chicago: Rand McNally, 1966.

71 Jones, Chester L. *Costa Rica and Civilization in the Caribbean.* New York: Russell & Russell, 1967.

Economics

72 Arias Sanchez, Oscar. "Barriers to Development in Costa Rica." *International Development Review* 15:2 (1973), 5-9.

73 DeWitt, R. Peter, Jr. *The Inter-American Development Bank and Political Influence: With Special Reference to Costa Rica.* New York: Praeger, 1977.

74 Hill, G. W. "The Agrarian Reform in Costa Rica." *Land Economics* 30 (Feb. 1964), 41-48.

75 May, Stacy, et al. *Costa Rica: A Study in Economic Development.* New York: Twentieth Century Fund, 1952.

76 McGovern, Joseph J. "The Costa Rica Labor Movement: A Study in Political Unionism." *Public and International Affairs* 4 (Spring 1966), 88-116.

Politics

Also see entry 230.

77 Acuña V., Miguel. *El 48.* San José: Liberia: Imprenta y Litografía Lehmann, 1974.

78 Ameringer, Charles D. *Don Pepé: A Political Biography of José Figueres of Costa Rica.* Albuquerque: University of New Mexico Press, 1978.

79 Bell, John P. *Crisis in Costa Rica: The 1948 Revolution.* Austin: University of Texas, Institute of Latin American Studies, 1971.

80 Busey, J. L. "Foundations of Political Contrast: Costa Rica and Nicaragua." *Western Political Quarterly* 11 (Sept. 1958), 627-659.

81 English, Burt H. *Liberacion Naciónal in Costa Rica: The Development of a Political Party in a Transitional Society.* Gainesville: University of Florida Press, 1971.

82 Kantor, Harry. *The Costa Rican Election of 1953: A Case Study.* Gainesville: University of Florida, Latin American Monographs, No. 5, 1958.

83 _____. "The Struggle for Democracy in Costa Rica." *South Atlantic Quarterly* 40 (Jan. 1956), 12-18.

84 Martz, John D. "Costa Rican Electoral Trends, 1953-1966." *Western Political Quarterly* 20 (Dec. 1967), 888-909.

85 Saxe-Fernandez, John. "The Militarization of Costa Rica." *Monthly Review* 24 (1972), 61-70.

86 Wells, Henry. "The 1970 Election in Costa Rica." *World Affairs* 133 (1970), 13-28.

Relations with Neighbors

87 Heath, Dwight B. "Costa Rica and Her Neighbors." *Current History* 58 (Feb. 1970), 95-101.

88 Salisbury, Richard V. "Costa Rica and the 1920-1921 Union Movement: a Reassessment." *Journal of Interamerican Studies and World Affairs* 19 (Aug. 1977), 393-418.

89 _____. "Domestic Politics and Foreign Policy: Costa Rica's Stand on Recognition, 1923-1934." *Hispanic American Historical Review* 54 (1974), 453-478.

Relations with U. S.

90 Baker, George W. "Woodrow Wilson's use of the Non-Recognition Policy in Costa Rica." *Americas* 22 (1965), 3-21.

91 Rippy, J. Fred. "Relations of the United States and Costa Rica during the Guardia Era." *Bulletin of the Pan American Union* 77 (1943), 61-68.

92 Stewart, Watt. *Keith and Costa Rica: A Biographical Study of Minor Cooper Keith.* Albuquerque: University of New Mexico Press, 1964.

EL SALVADOR

The only adequate survey of Salvadoran history in English is Alastair White's *El Salvador* [entry 95]. Other studies emphasize important topics, such as Thomas Anderson's *Matanza* [entry 103] which is an excellent analysis of the 1932 rebellion and government suppression thereof. Robert Elam's dissertation "Appeal to Arms" [entry 104] illustrates the importance of the military in Salvadoran politics. For the 1969 "Soccer War" with Honduras see [entries 220 through 223].

Foreign Policy's "El Salvador: The Current Danger" [entry 114] provides a good introduction to the dimension of that country's contemporary crisis. Two sympathetic views of the rebel cause, and condemnations of U.S. policy towards El Salvador are Cynthia Arnson [entry 123] and Tommie Sue Montgomery [entry 119]. A more balanced account providing excellent background material is Enrique Baloyra's *El Salvador in Transition* [entry 112]. An argument for letting the rebel groups into the power structure is Piero Gleijeses' "The Case for Power Sharing in El Salvador" [entry 117].

General

93 Blutstein, Howard I. et.al. *El Salvador: A Country Study.* Washington, D.C.: G.P.O., 1979.

94 Osborne, Lilly de Jongh. *Four Keys to El Salvador.* New York: Funk & Wagnalls, 1956.

95 White, Alastair. *El Salvador.* New York: Praeger, 1973.

Economics

96 Brooks, Joseph J. "The Impact of U.S. Cotton Policy on Economic Development: The Cases of El Salvador and Nicaragua." *Public and International Affairs* 5 (Spring 1967), 191-214.

97 Gordon, Jerome B. "Labor Mobility and Economic Growth: The Central American Experience: Costa Rica and El Salvador." *Economic Development and Cultural Change* 17 (Apr. 1969), 319-337.

98 "New Legislation on Agricultural Labour in El Salvador." *International Labour Review* 85 (Mar. 1962), 294-299.

99 Oldman, Oliver. "Tax Reform in El Salvador." *Inter-American Law Review.* (July 1964), 379-420.

100 Simon, Laurence and James Stephens. *El Salvador Land Reform 1980-1981.* Boston: Oxfam Americs, 1981.

101 Wilford, D. Sykes and Walton T. Wilford. *Monetary Policy, Credit Institutions, and Argicultural Credit in El Salvador.* San Salvador: Agency for International Development, 1975.

Politics

102 Anderson, Charles W. "El Salvador: The Army as Reformer." In *Political Systems of Latin America.* Edited by Martin C. Needler. New York: Van Nostrand, 1970.

103 Anderson, Thomas P. *Matanza: El Salvador's Communist Revolt of 1932.* Lincoln: University of Nebraska Press, 1971.

104 Elam, Robert V. "Appeal to Arms: The Army and Politics in El Salvador, 1931-1964." Ph.D. Dissertation. New Mexico: University of New Mexico, 1968.

105 Handal, Shafik J. "El Salvador: A Precarious Balance." *World Marxist Review* 16 (June 1973), 46-50.

106 Lemus, José Maria. *Pueblo ejercito y doctrina revolucionaria.* San Salvador: Ministeria del Interior, 1952.

107 McDonald, Ronald H. "Electoral Behavior and Political Development in El Salvador." *Journal of Politics* 31 (May 1969), 397-419.

108 Sánchez, J. "Social Developments in El Salvador and the Policy of the Communist Party." *World Marxist Review* 8 (Aug. 1965), 11-16.

109 Webre, Stephen. *José Napoléon Duarte and the Christian Democratic Party in El Salvadoran Politics, 1960-1972.* Baton Rouge: Lousiana State University Press, 1974.

110 Woosley, Lawrence H. "Recognition of the Government of El Salvador." *American Journal of International Law* 28 (1934), 325-329.

Contemporary Crisis

111 Armstrong, Robert and Janet Shenk. *El Salvador: The Face of Revolution.* Boston: South End Press, 1982.

112 Baloyra, Enrique. *El Salvador in Transition.* Chapel Hill: University of North Carolina Press, 1982.

113 Bonpane, Blaise. "Understanding the Salvadoran Revolutionaries." *Center Magazine* 14 (Nov./Dec. 1981), 57-64.

114 "El Salvador: The Current Danger." (symposium). *Foreign Policy* 43 (Summer 1981), 71-88.

115 "El Salvador - Why Revolution." *NACLA Report on the Americas.* New York: NACLA, 1980.

116 Gettlemen, Marvin, et.al. *El Salvador: Central America in the New Cold War.* New York: Grove Press, 1981.

117 Gleijeses, Piero. "The Case for Power Sharing in El Salvador." *Foreign Affairs* 61 (Summer 1983), 1048-63.

118 Macoin, G. "Longstanding Oppression is the Cause of El Salvador's Civil War." *Center Magazine* 14 (Nov./Dec. 1981), 47-56.

119 Montgomery, Tommie Sue. *Revolution in El Salvador: Origins and Evolution.* Boulder, CO: Westview, 1982.

120 North, Lisa. *Bitter Grounds, Roots of the Revolt in El Salvador.* Toronto: Between the Lines, 1981.

121 Organization of American States. *Report on the Situation of Human Rights in El Salvador.* Washington, D.C.: General Secretariat of the OAS, 1979.

122 White, Robert E. "There is no Military Solution in El Salvador." *Center Magazine* 14 (July/Aug. 1981), 5-13.

Relations with U. S.

Salvador's current crisis cannot be separated from United States interests; under **United States—Central American Relations** see "Contemporary Crisis" [entries 365 through 387] and "Policy Recommendations" [entries 396 through 402].

123 Arnson, Cynthia. *El Salvador: A Revolution Confronts the United States.* Washington, D.C.: Institute for Policy Studies, 1982.

124 Commission on United States-Central American Relations. *El Salvador: America's War Without Honor.* Washington, D.C.: Center for Development Policy, 1984.

125 Devine, Frank J. *El Salvador: Embassy Under Attack.* New York: Vantage Press, 1981.

126 Grieb, Kenneth J. "The U. S. and the Rise of General Maximiliano Hernández Martínez." *Journal of Latin American Studies* 3 (Nov. 1971), 151-172.

127 "On U.S. Relations with El Salvador: The Koch-State Department Correspondence." *Inter-American Economic Affairs* 30 (Summer 1976), 79-83.

128 United States. Congress. House Committee on International Relations. Subcommittee on Inter-American Affairs. *The Recent Presidential Elections in El Salvador: Implications for U.S. Foreign Policy.* 95th Congress, 1st Session. Washington, D.C.: G.P.O., 1977.

GUATEMALA

Guatemala's central role in the region's history is reflected by the abundance of literature dealing with the republic. Still, a recent historical analysis is lacking. Standard histories include those by Amy Elizabeth Jensen, Chester Lloyd Jones, Joan Lloyd and Nathan Whetten [entries 131, 132, 133 and 135].

The dictatorship of Jorge Ubico is sympathetically studied by Kenneth J. Grieb, *Guatemalan Caudillo* [entry 141]. To understand the controversial Arévalo, one must rely largely on his own works [entries 136 through 139], all but one in Spanish. Together, they provide an understanding of his "Spiritual Socialism." The question of communist influence in government during Arévalo's administration is covered by Ronald Schneider's *Communism in Guatemala* [entry 166], which is based upon Guatemalan sources. Ralph Lee Woodward's article "Octubre: Communist Appeal to the Urban Labor Force of Guatemala," [entry 172] is also helpful.

Landowning patterns are often described as the root cause of Guatemala's economic and political problems. Thomas and Marjorie Melville's *Guatemala: The Politics of Land Ownership* [entry 151] is an excellent analysis. Much briefer, but equally as good, is David McCreery's "Coffee and Class: The Structure of Development in Guatemala" [entry 150].

Guatemala became the focus of alleged Soviet penetration in the early post-World War II period, and resulted in the U. S. sponsored invasion of the country in 1954 to oust the Arbenz regime. The official U. S. position is explained in two government publications [entries 192 and 193]. However, Richard Immerman's recent study, *The C.I.A. in Guatemala* refutes the government's allegation [entry 186], as does entry 190a.

General

129 Adams, Richard N. *Crucifixion by Power.* Austin: University of Texas Press, 1970.

130 Holleran, Mary P. *Church and State in Guatemala.* New York: Columbia University Press, 1949.

131 Jensen, Amy E. *Guatemala: A Historical Survey.* New York: Exposition Press, 1955.

132 Jones, Chester L. *Guatemala: Past and Present.* Minneapolis: University of Minnesota Press, 1940.

133 Lloyd, Joan. *Guatemala, Land of the Mayas.* London: Travel Book Club, 1965.

134 Myrop, Richard F., et. al. *Guatemala: A Country Study.* Washington, D.C.: G.P.O., 1984.

135 Whetten, Nathan. *Guatemala: The Land and the People.* New Haven: Yale University Press, 1961.

Biography

136 Arevalo, Juan José. *Anti-Kommunsim in Latin America.* New York: Lyle Stuart, 1963.

137 _____. *Guatemala: la democracia y el imperio.* Buenos Aires: Editorial Palestra, 1964.

138 _____. *La inquietual normalista.* San Salvador: Editorial Universitaria, 1970.

139 _____. *The Shark and the Sardines.* Trans. by June Cobb and Raul Osequeda. New York: Lyle Stuart (1956), 1961.

140 Cospín, Miguel Angel. *Ydígoras Fuentes ante la faz de sus contemporaneos.* Mexico, D.F.: Costa-Amic, 1970.

141 Grieb, Kenneth J. *Guatemalan Caudillo: The Regime of Jorge Ubico, Guatemala 1931-1944.* Athens: Ohio University Press, 1978.

142 Raine, Alice. *Eagle of Guatemala: Justo Rufino Barrios.* New York: Harcourt, Brace, 1947.

143 Ydigoras Fuentes, Miguel, with Mario Rosenthal. *My War with Communism.* Englewood Cliffs, N.J.: Prentice-Hall, 1963.

Economics

144 Bauer Paiz, Alfonso. *Como opera el capital yanqui en Centroamérica: El Caso de Guatemala.* Mexico,D.F.: Editora Iberoamericana, 1956.

145 Bishop, Edwin W. *The Guatemalan Labor Movement, 1944-1959.* Madison: University of Wisconsin Press, 1959.

146 Branno, Russell H. *Coffee: A Background Study with Primary Emphasis in Guatemala.* Madison: University of Wisconsin, The Land Tenure Center, 1964.

147 Fletcher, Lehman B., et. al. *Guatemala's Economic Development: The Role of Agriculture.* Ames: Iowa State University Press, 1971.

148 Hoy, Don R. "A Review of Development Planning in Guatemala." *Journal of Inter-American Studies* 12 (Apr. 1970), 217-228.

149 Hoyt, Elizabeth E. "The Indian Laborer on Guatemalan Coffee Fincas." *Inter-American Economic Affairs* 9 (Summer 1955), 33-46.

150 McCreery, David J. "Coffee and Class: The Structure of Development in Liberal Guatemala." *Hispanic American Historical Review* 56 (Aug. 1976), 438-460.

151 Melville, Thomas and Marjorie Melville. *Guatemala: The Politics of Land Ownership.* New York: Free Press, 1971.

152 Mosk, Sanford A. "The Coffee Economy of Guatemala, 1850-1918." *Inter-American Economic Affairs* 9 (Winter 1955), 6-20.

153 Schmid, Lester. "The Productivity of Agricultural Labor in the Export Crops of Guatemala." *Inter-American Economic Affairs* 22 (Autumn, 1968), 33-46.

Politics

154 Castro, José Rafael. *Politica international de Guatemala, 1944-1957.* Havana: Imprint "H.C.," 1957.

155 De La Souchere, Elena. "Guatemala: No Communist Bridgehead." *Monthly Review* 6 (July 1954), 102-115.

156 Fried, Jonathan, et.al. *Guatemala in Rebellion: Unfinished History.* New York: Grove Press, 1983.

157 Galeano, Eduardo. *Guatemala: Occupied Country.* New York: Monthly Review Press, 1969.

158 Gillin, John and K.H. Silvert. "Ambiguities in Guatemala." *Foreign Affairs* 34 (Apr. 1966), 469-482.

159 Gilly, Aldolfo. "The Guerrilla Movement in Guatemala." *Monthly Review* 17 (May 1965), 9-40; (June 1965), 7-41.

160 Grunewald, Donald. "The Anglo-Guatemalan Dispute Over British Honduras." *Caribbean Studies* 5 (July 1965), 17-44.

161 "Guatemala: Breaking Free." *NACLA's Latin America and Empire Report* 8 (Mar. 1974), 1-23.

162 Johnson, Kenneth F. "On the Guatemalan Political Violence." *Politics and Society* 4 (Fall 1973), 55-82.

163 Lujan, Herman D. "Structure of Political Support: A Study of Guatemala." *American Journal of Political Science* 18 (Feb. 1974), 23-43.

164 Millett, Richard. "The Politics of Violence: Guatemala and El Salvador." *Current History* 80 (Feb. 1980), 70-74ffl.

165 Roberts, Bryan. "Urban Poverty and Political Behavior in Guatemala." *Human Organization* 29 (Spring 1970), 20-28.

166 Schneider, Ronald M. *Communism in Guatemala, 1944-1954.* New York: Praeger, 1958.

167 Simons, M. "Guatemala: The Coming Danger." *Foreign Policy* 43 (Summer 1981), 93-103.

168 Sloan, John. "Electoral Power Contenders in Guatemala." *Caribbean Studies* 11 (Oct. 1971), 19-34.

169 _____. "The 1966 Presidential Election in Guatemala." *Inter-American Economic Affairs* 22 (Autumn 1968), 15-32.

170 Organization of American States. *Report on the Situation of Human Rights in the Republic of Guatemala.* Washington, D.C.: General Secretariat of the OAS, 1981.

171 Weiner, Peter H. "Guatemala: The Aborted Revolution." *The Harvard Review* 4 (Summer 1966), 35-48.

172 Woodward, Ralph Lee, Jr. "Octubre: Communist Appeal to the Urban Labor Force of Guatemala: 1950-1953." *Journal of Inter-American Studies* 4 (July 1962), 363-374.

Relations with U.S.

173 Baker, George W., Jr. "The Woodrow Wilson Administration and Guatemalan Relations." *Historian* 27 (1965), 155-169.

174 Grieb, Kenneth J. "America's Involvement in the Rise of Jorge Ubico." *Caribbean Studies* 10 (Apr. 1970), 5-21.

175 _____. "Negotiating a Reciprocal Trade Agreement with an Under-developed Country: Guatemala as a Case Study." *Prologue* 5 (1973), 22-29.

176 Jenkins, Brian and Caesar D. Sereseres. "U.S. Military Assistance and the Guatemalan Armed Forces." *Armed Forces and Society* 3 (Summer 1977), 575-594.

177 McLaughlin, Robert T. "The Peace Corps in Guatemala." *Public and International Affairs* 4 (Spring 1966), 36-65.

178 Rippy, J. Fred. "Relations of the United States and Guatemala during the Epoch of Justo Rufino Barrios." *Hispanic American Historical Review* 22 (1942), 595-605.

179 "Situation in Guatemala." *U.S. Department of State Bulletin* 81 (Oct. 1981), 79-81.

180 United States. Congress. House Committee on Foreign Affairs. *Report of the Special Study Mission to Guatemala.* Washington, D.C.: G.P.O., 1957.

181 United States. Congress. Senate Committee on Foreign Relations. Subcommittee on Western Hemisphere Affairs. *Guatemala and the Dominican Republic.* Washington, D.C.: G.P.O., 1971.

182 United States. Department of the Army. Civic Action Branch, Civil Affairs Directorate. *Military Civic Action Program in Guatemala, Ecuador and Colombia.* Washington, D.C.: Department of the Army, 1964.

183 Woodward, Ralph L., Jr. "Guatemalan Cotton and the American Civil War." *Inter-American Economic Affairs* 18 (Winter 1964), 87-94.

U.S. Intervention

184 Ayhn de Soto, José M. *Dependency and Intervention: The Case of Guatemala in 1954.* Boulder, CO: Westview, 1978.

185 Gordon, Max. "A Case History of U. S. Subversion: Guatemala, 1954." *Science and Society* 35 (Summer 1971), 129-155.

186 Immerman, Richard H. *The CIA in Guatemala: The Foreign Policy of Intervention.* Austin: University of Texas Press, 1982.

187 McDermott, Louis M. "Guatemala 1954: Intervention and Aggression?" *Rocky Mountain Social Science Journal* 9 (Jan. 1972), 79-88.

188 Peurifoy, J. E. "The Communist Conspiracy in Guatemala." *U.S. Department of State Bulletin* 31 (Nov. 8, 1954), 690-696.

189 _____. "Meeting the Communist Challenge in the Western Hemisphere." *U.S. Department of State Bulletin* 31 (Sept. 6, 1957), 333-336.

190 Pike, Frederick B. "Guatemala, the United States and Communism in the Americas." *Review of Politics* 17 (1955), 232-261.

190a Schlesinger, Stephen and Stephen Kinzer. *Bitter Fruit: The Untold Story of the American Coup in Guatemala.* Garden City, N.Y.: Doubleday, 1982.

191 Taylor, Philip B., Jr. "The Guatemala Affair: A Critique of U.S. Foreign Policy." *American Political Science Review* 50 (Sept. 1956), 787-806.

192 United States. Department of State. *A Case History of Communist Penetration in Guatemala.* Washington, D.C.: G.P.O., 1957.

193 United States. Department of State. *Intervention of International Communism in Guatemala.* Washington, D.C.: G.P.O., 1954.

HONDURAS

The most significant work on Honduran history in English is James A. Morris, *Honduras: Caudillo Politics and Military Rulers* [entry 209]. An important earlier study is William Stokes' *Honduras: An Area Study in Government* [entry 199]. Among the better studies in Spanish is José Martínez *Honduras Historica* [entry 197]. Steve Ropp's "The Honduran Army" [entry 213] best illustrates the dominance of the military in post-World War II politics. It should be balanced with Ramón Villeda Morales' defense of the military in its struggle against communism [entry 215]. The impact of the 1969 "Soccer War" is best discussed by Thomas P. Anderson, *The War of The Dispossessed* [entry 220].

General

194 Alvarado R., Martín. *La enseñanza de la historia en Honduras.* Mexico, D.F.: Instituto Panamericano de geografía e historia, 1951.

195 Charles, Cecil. *Honduras: The Land of Great Depths.* Chicago: Rand McNally, 1890.

196 Lombard, Thomas R. *The New Honduras: Its Situation, Resources, Opportunities, and Prospects, concisely stated from recent personal observations.* New York: Brentanos, 1887.

197 Martínez, José F. *Honduras historica.* Tegucigalpa: Imprenta Nacional, 1974.

198 Rudolph, James D. *Honduras: A Country Study.* Washington, D.C.: G.P.O., 1984.

199 Stokes, William S. *Honduras: An Area Study in Government.* Madison: University of Wisconsin Press, 1950.

200 Vivas, Rafael Leivas. *Honduras: fuerzas armadas.* Tegucigalpa: Universidad Nacional Autónoma de Honduras, 1973.

Economics

201 "Agrarian Reform Law in Honduras." *International Labour Review* 87 (June 1963), 573-580.

202 Becerra, Longino. *El problema agrario en Honduras.* La Habana: Casa de las Américas, 1964.

203 Checchi, Vincent. *Honduras: A Problem in Economic Development.* New York: Twentieth Century Fund, 1959.

204 La Barge, Richard A. and Frank Falero, Jr. "Fifteen Years of Banking in Honduras." *Journal of Inter-American Studies* 9 (Oct. 1967), 448-506.

205 Morris, James A. and Steve C. "Corporatism and Dependent Development: A Honduran Case Study." *Latin American Research Review* 12 (Fall 1977), 27-68.

206 Parsons, Kenneth H. "Agrarian Reform in Southern Honduras." Madison: University of Wisconsin Press, Land Tenure Center, 1975.

207 Shepherd, Robert. "Honduras: A Land of Promise." *Industrial Development and Manufacturer's Record* 133 (Nov. 1964), 21-52.

208 Stokes, William S. "Honduras: Dilemma of Development." *Current History* 42 (Feb. 1962), 83-88.

Politics

209 Morris, James A. *Honduras: Caudillo Politics and Military Rulers.* Boulder, CO: Westview, 1984.

210 Muñoz, Alonzo. "The People of Honduras in the Fight Against Reaction and Imperialism." *World Marxist Review* 7 (June 1964), 24-28.

211 Padilla, Rigoberto. "The Collapse of Bourgeois Reformism and the Communist Alternative." *World Marxist Review* 20 (Nov. 1977), 85-91.

212 Paredes, Lucas. *Liberalismo y nacionalismo.* Tegucigalpa: Imprenta Honduras, 1963.

213 Ropp, Steve C. "The Honduran Army and the Socio-political Evolution of the Honduran State." *The Americas* 30 (Apr. 1974), 504-528.

214 Rosenberg, Mark B. "Nicaragua and Honduras: Toward Garrison States." *Current History* 83 (Feb. 1984) 59-62ff.

215 Villeda Morales, Ramón. *La defensa de la democracia frente a la amenaza communista* [The defense of democracy against the communist menace]. Tegucigalpa: Imprenta Nacional, 1969.

Relations with U. S.

Honduras has become a focal point in current U. S. policy toward the region. Under **United States—Central American Relations** see "Contemporary Crisis" [entries 365 through 387] and "Policy Recommendations" [entries 396 through 402].

216 Baker, George W., Jr. "Ideas and Realities in the Wilson Administration's Relations with Honduras." *Americas* 21 (1964), 3-19.

217 Bosworth, S. W. "Recent Developments in Honduras." *U.S. Department of State Bulletin* 82 (Nov. 1982), 60-63.

218 Wheaton, Philip E. *Inside Honduras: Regional Counterinsurgency Base.* Washington, D.C.: EPICA Task Force, 1982.

219 _____. *The Iron Triangle: The Honduran Connection.* Washington, D.C.: EPICA Task Force, 1981.

Honduras—El Salvador War, 1969

220 Anderson, Thomas P. *The War of The Dispossessed: Honduras and El Salvador.* Lincoln: University of Nebraska Press, 1983.

221 Carías, Marco V. *Análisis del conflicto entre Honduras y El Salvador.* Tegucigalpa: Universidad Nacional Autónoma de Honduras Facultad de Ciencias y Economías, 1969.

222 Mallin, Jay. "Military Affairs Abroad: Salvador-Honduras War, 1969." *Air University Review* 21 (Mar. 1970), 87-92.

223 "A Microscopic View of The O.A.S.: The Honduras-El Salvador Conflict." *Virginia Law Review* 57 (Mar. 1970), 291-314.

NICARAGUA

An adequate overview of Nicaraguan history is Thomas W. Walker's *Nicaragua: The Land of Sandino* [entry 230]. Those publishied in Spanish such as José Gáme , Alejandro Cole Chamarro and Ricardo Castillo Paiz [entries 225, 226 and 227] are highly nationalistic. The Somoza regime has received most attention. Three important works include Eduardo Crawley's *Dictators Never Die: A Portrait of Nicaragua and the Somozas* [entry 226], Bernard Diederich, *Somoza and the Legacy of United States Involvement in Central America* [entry 236], and Richard Millett, *Guardians of the Dynasty* [entry 243]. They all point to the use of the National Guard as the Somoza's prop of support, the family's control of the economy and political machinery, and the reliance on friendship with the United States.

Important studies of earlier periods include Neill Macaulay's *The Sandino Affair* [entry 242], and Charles Stansifer's "José Santos Zelaya" [entry 233]. Both are sympathetic accounts of important Nicaraguan political figures.

United States intervention in Nicaragua prior to the Somoza dynasty is critically examined by Joseph O. Baylen and William Kamman [entries 255 and 259].

General

224 Ayon, Tomás. *Historia de Nicaragua.* Managua: Banco de América, 1977.

225 Chamorro, Alejandro Cole. *145 años* de historia politica: Nicaragua. Managua: Editorial Nicaraguence, 1967.

226 Gámez, José D. *Historia Moderna de Nicaragua.* Managua: Banco de América, 1975.

227 Paiz Castillo, Ricardo. *Historia de Nicaragua.* León: Editorial Hospicio, 1964.

228 Rudolph, James D. et.al. *Nicaragua: A Country Study.* Washington, D.C.: G.P.O., 1982.

229 Stout, Peter F. *Nicaragua: Past, Present, and Future.* Philadelphia: John E. Potter, 1859.

230 Walker, Thomas W. *Nicaragua: The Land of Sandino.* Boulder, CO.: Westview, 1982.

Biographies

231 Selser, Gregorio. *Sandino.* New York: Monthly Review, 1982.

232 Squier, E. George. *Adventures on the Mosquito Shore.* Chicago: Belgord, 1888.

233 Stansifer, Charles L. "José Santos Zelaya: A New Look at Nicaragua's 'Liberal' Dictator." *Interamericana/Inter-American Review* 7 (Fall 1977), 460-480.

The Somozas

234 Chamorro Cadenal, Pedro J. *Estripe Sangrienta: Los Somoza.* Mexico, D.F.: Patria y Libertad, 1957.

235 Crawley, Eduardo. *Dictators Never Die: A Portrait of Nicaragua and the Somozas.* New York: St. Martin's, 1979.

236 Diederich, Bernard. *Somoza and the Legacy of United States Involvement in Central America.* New York: Dutton, 1981.

237 Halftermeyer, Gratus. *El General Anastasio Somoza, su vida y su obra.* Managua: Nacional Imprenta, 1957.

238 Peterson, J. A. "Somoza vs. the Americans." *Nation* 168 (1949), 63-66.

Economics and Politics

Also see entries 80 and 96.

239 Busey, J. L. "Foundations of Political Contrasts: Costa Rica and Nicaragua." *Western Political Quarterly* 11 (Sept. 1958), 627-659.

240 Chamorro Cardenal, Pedro J. *Diario de un preso.* Managua: Editorial Nuevos Horizontes, 1963.

241 Kleiner, Karol C. *Labor Law and Practice in Nicaragua.* Washington, D.C.: U.S. Department of Labor, Bureau of Labor Statistics, 1964.

242 Macaulay, Neill. *The Sandino Affair.* Chicago: Quadrangle, 1967.

243 Millet, Richard. *Guardians of the Dynasty.* Maryknoll, NY: ORBIS, 1977.

244 Swenson, Walter. *Cost of Production Analysis of the Major Food Crops of Nicaragua.* Columbia: University of Missouri Press, 1974.

245 Walker, Thomas W. *The Christian Democratic Movement in Nicaragua.* Tucson: University of Arizona Press, 1970.

Sandinist Revolution

The most balanced account of the events since 1972 that resulted in Somoza's downfall is John Booth's *The End and the Beginning* [entry 246], which clearly illustrates the coalescing of Nicaragua's several political and social factions against the dictator. William M. Leo Grande [entry 249] discusses the confusion Americans have over the meaning of communism in Central America. Also see CONTEMPORARY CRISIS [entries 365 through 387] and POLICY RECOMMENDATIONS [entries 396 through 402] under **United States-Central American Relations.**

246 Booth, John A. *The End and The Beginning: The Nicaraguan Revolution.* Boulder, CO: Westview, 1982.

247 Cruz, Arturo J. "Nicaragua's Imperiled Revolution." *Foreign Affairs* 61 (Summer 1983), 1031-1047.

248 Fagen, Richard R. "Dateline Nicaragua: The End of the Affair." *Foreign Policy* 36 (Fall 1979), 178-191.

249 Leo Grande, William M. "Revolution in Nicaragua: Another Cuba?" *Foreign Affairs* 58 (Fall 1979), 178-191.

250 *Nicaragua: A People's Revolution.* Washingtion, D.C.: EPICA Task Force, 1980.

251 "Nicaragua: Symposium." *U.S. Department of State Bulletin* 79 (Aug. 1979), 55-62.

252 Somoza, Anastasio as told to Jack Cox. *Nicaragua Betrayed.* Boston: Western Islands, 1980.

253 Weber, Henri. *Nicaragua: The Sandinist Revolution.* New York: Schocken, 1982.

254 Walker, Thomas W. "Nicaragua Consolidated Its Revolution." *Current History* 80 (Feb. 1981) 79-82 +.

Relations with U. S.

Under the subheading *NINETEENTH CENTURY* of **United States—Central American Relations** see entries 277, 278 and 285 for a discussion of William Walker's filibustering activities. See entries 300, 301, 302, 303, 305 and 311 for a discussion of the proposed interoceanic canal route through Nicaragua.

255 Baker, George W., Jr. "The Wilson Administration and Nicaragua, 1913-1921." *Americas* 22 (1966), 339-376.

256 Baylen, J. O. "American Intervention in Nicaragua, 1909-33: An Appraisal of Objectives and Results." *Southwestern Social Science Quarterly* 35 (1954), 128-154.

257 Cox, Isaac J. *Nicaragua and the United States, 1909-1927.* Boston: World Peace Foundation, 1927.

258 Denny, Harold. *Dollars for Bullets: The Story of American Rule in Nicaragua.* New York: Dial, 1929.

259 Greer, Virginia L. "State Department Policy in Regard to the Nicaraguan Election of 1924." *Hispanic American Historical Review* 34 (1954), 445-67.

260 Kamman, William. *A Search for Stability: United States Diplomacy toward Nicaragua, 1925-1933.* Notre Dame: University of Notre Dame Press, 1968.

261 Koch, Edward. "The Koch-State Department Correspondence on U.S. Relations with Nicaragua." *Inter-American Economic Affairs* 29 (1976), 85-93.

262 Organization of American States. *Report on the Situation of Human Rights in Nicaragua.* Washington, D.C.: General Secretariat of the OAS, 1978.

263 Stimson, Henry L. *American Policy in Nicaragua.* New York: Scribner's, 1927.

264 Tierney, John J., Jr. "U. S. Intervention in Nicaragua, 1927-1933: Lessons for Today." *Orbis* 14:4 (1971), 1012-28.

265 United States. Department of State. *The United States and Nicaragua: A Survey of the Relations from 1909 to 1932.* Washington, D.C.: G.P.O., 1932.

United States-Central American Relations

Currently there are no studies focusing solely on United States diplomatic relations with Central America. Thus, one must turn to studies of United States relations with the Caribbean, and with Latin America. The most significant works covering Caribbean relations are two volumes by Lester D. Langley. The first, *Struggle for the American Mediterranian* [entry 269] covers the nineteenth century and emphasizes rivalry with the British. The second, *The United States and the Caribbean, 1900-1970* [entry 270] focuses upon the U.S. effort to establish political hegemony over the region.

Analysis of overall United States-Latin American relations are useful for studying the region within the context of larger hemispheric policies. J. Lloyd Mecham's, *A Survey of United States-Latin American Relations* [entry 272] and Graham Stuart and James L. Tigner's *Latin America and the United States* [entry 275] include more material on the Caribbean basin region than the other general histories.

The *Foreign Relations Series* [entry 276] is very uneven in its treatment of Central America, particularly in the nineteenth century. The selected documents emphasize political developments.

266 Bemis, Samuel Flagg. *The Latin American Policy of the United States: An Historical Interpretation.* New York: Harcourt Brace, 1943.

267 Burr, Robert. *Our Troubled Hemisphere: Perspectives on United States-Latin American Relations.* Washington, D.C.: Brookings Institution, 1967.

268 Connell-Smith, Gordon. *The United States and Latin America: An Historical Analysis of Inter-American Relations.* New York: Wiley, 1974.

269 Langley, Lester D. *The United States and the Caribbean 1900-1970.* Athens: University of Georgia Press, 1980.

270 _____. *Struggle for the American Mediterranean.* Athens: University of Georgia Press, 1976.

271 Lieuwen, Edwin. *United States Policy in Latin America: A Short History.* New York: Praeger, 1965.

272 Mecham, J. Lloyd. *A Survey of United States-Latin American Relations.* Boston: Houghton Mifflin, 1965.

273 Perkins, Dexter. *The United States And the Caribbean.* Cambridge: Harvard University Press, 1966.

274 Rippy, J. Fred. *The Caribbean Danger Zone.* New York: Putnam's, 1940.

275 Stuart, Graham and James L. Tigner. *Latin America and the United States.* Englewood Cliffs, NJ: Prentice-Hall, 1975.

276 United States. Department of State. *Foreign Relations of the United States.* Washington, D.C.: G.P.O., 1860-1984.

NINETEETH CENTURY

A dated, but useful study of United States-Central American relations from independence until the twentieth century, is Dana G. Munro's *Five Republics of Central America* [entry 286]. The changing American attitude toward world affairs in the latter part of the nineteenth century is examined by Walter LaFeber in his *New Empire* [entry 283], which places emphasis upon economics. This should be balanced with Charles S. Campbell's *The Transformation of American Foreign Relations, 1865-1900* [entry 281]. The filibustering activities of William Walker into Central America during the 1850s is best analyzed by Albert Z. Carr [entry 278]. The titles under ANGLO-AMERICAN RELATIONS [entries 287 through 299] and TRANSISTHMIAN CANAL [entries 300 through 313] below are useful.

277 Allen, Merritt. *William Walker, Filibuster.* New York: Harper, 1932.

278 Carr, Albert Z. *The World and William Walker.* New York: Harper & Row, 1963.

279 Deutsch, Hermann B. *The Incredible Yanqui: The Career of Lee Christmas.* New York: Longmans, Green, 1931.

280 Feipel, Louis N. "The Navy and Filibustering in the Fifties." *U.S. Naval Institute Proceedings* 44 (1918), 767 ff.

281 Campbell, Charles S. *The Transformation of American Foreign Relations 1865-1900.* New York: Harper & Row, 1976.

282 Humphreys, R. A. *The Diplomatic History of British Honduras, 1638-1901.* London: Oxford University Press, 1961.

283 LaFeber, Walter. *New Empire: An Interpretation of American Expansion, 1860-1898.* Ithaca, NY: Cornell University Press, 1963.

284 Manning, William R., ed. *Diplomatic Correspondence of the United States: Inter-American Affairs, 1831-1860.* 12 vols. Washington, D.C.: Carneige Endowment for International Peace, 1932-1939.

285 May, Robert E. *The Southern Dream of a Caribbean Empire: 1854-1861.* Baton Rouge: Louisiana State University Press, 1973.

286 Munro, Dana G. *Five Republics of Central America: Their Political and Economic Development and Their Relations with the United States.* New York: Oxford University Press, 1918.

ANGLO-AMERICAN RELATIONS

The Anglo-American rivalry which dominated the early part of the nineteenth century is best covered by Wilbur Jones in *The American Problem in British Diplomacy* [entry 291] and Mario Rodríguez in *A Palmerstonian Diplomat in Central America* [entry 295]. The controversy over the 1850 Clayton-Bulwer Treaty is covered by Kenneth Bourne [entry 287] and Richard Van Alstyne [entry 298]. Bourne describes the treaty as affectively limiting British interests in the area, while Van Alstyne takes the opposite view; namely, that U.S. interests were limited.

287 Bourne, Kenneth. "The Clayton-Bulwer Treaty and the Decline of British Opposition to the Territorial Expansion of the United States, 1857-1860." *Journal of Modern History* 33 (1961), 287-291.

288 Great Britain. Parliament, House of Commons. *British Parliamentary Papers United States of America.* Vol 15:2. *Correspondence Respecting American and British Affairs in Central and South America, 1850-1896.* Shannon: Irish University Press, 1971.

289 Hickson, G. E. "Palmerston and the Clayton-Bulwer Treaty." *Cambridge Historical Journal* 3 (1931), 295-303.

290 Howe, George F. "The Clayton-Bulwer Treaty." *American Historical Review* 42 (1937), 484-490.

291 Jones, Wilbur D. *The American Problem in British Diplomacy, 1841-1861.* Athens: University of Georgia Press, 1974.

292 Naylor, Robert A. "The British Role in Central America prior to the Clayton-Bulwer Treaty of 1850." *Hispanic American Historical Review* 40 (Aug. 1960), 361-382.

293 Neale, Robert G. *Great Britain and United States Expansion: 1898-1900.* East Lansing: Michigan State University Press, 1966.

294 Rippy, J. Fred. *British Investment in Latin America, 1822-1949.* Hamden, CT: Archon, 1966.

295 Rodríguez, Mario. *A Palmerstonian Diplomat in Central America: Frederick Chatfield, Esq.* Tucson: University of Arizona Press, 1964.

296 _____. "The Promethus and the Clayton-Bulwer Treaty." *Journal of Modern History* 36 (Sept. 1964), 260-278.

297 Van Aken, Mark. "British Policy Considerations in Central America before 1850." *Hispanic American Historical Review* 42 (1962), 54-59.

298 Van Alstyne, Richard W. "British Diplomacy and the Clayton-Bulwer Treaty, 1850-1860." *Journal of Modern History* 11 (1939), 149-183.

299 _____. "The Central American Policy of Lord Palmerston, 1846-1848." *Hispanic American Historical Review* 16 (1936), 339-359.

TRANSISTHMIAN CANAL

The building of the Panama Canal increased United States interest in isthmian affairs. The works by Miles P. Du Val, E. Taylor Parks and Mary W. Williams [entries 303, 310 and 313] best describe the political and diplomatic history of the canal. Following the canal's construction, United States—Panamanian relations are important for understanding U. S. attitudes toward the isthmian region. For this purpose see Lawrence O. Ealy and Walter LaFeber [entries 304 and 306].

300 Allen, Cyril. *France in Central America: Felix Belly and the Nicaragua Canal.* New York: Pageant, 1966.

301 Bailey, Thomas A. "Interest in a Nicaragua Canal, 1903-1931." *Hispanic American Historical Review* 16 (1936), 2-28.

302 Crowell, Jackson. "The U.S. and a Central American Canal, 1869-1877." *Hispanic American HISTORICAL Review* 49 (Feb. 1969), 27-52.

303 Du Val, Miles P. *Cadiz to Cathay; the Story of the Long Diplomatic Struggle for the Panama Canal.* New York: Greenwood (1947), 1968.

304 Ealy, Lawrence O. *Yanqui Politics and the Isthmian Canal.* University Park: Pennsylvania State University Press, 1971.

305 Folkman, David I., Jr. *The Nicaragua Route.* Salt Lake City: University of Utah Press, 1972.

306 LaFeber, Walter. *The Panama Canal: The Crisis in Historical Perspective.* New York: Oxford University Press, 1976.

307 Lockey, Joseph B. "Diplomatic Futility." *Hispanic American Historical Review* 10 (1930), 265-294.

308 _____. "A Neglected Aspect of Isthmian Diplomacy." *American Historical Review* 41 (1936), 295-305.

309 Mack, Gerstle. *The Land Divided: A History of the Panama Canal and other Isthmian Canal Projects.* New York: Knopf, 1944.

310 Parks, E. Taylor. *Colombia and the United States, 1765-1934.* Durham, NC: Duke University Press, 1935.

311 Scheips, Paul F. "United States Commercial Pressures for a Nicaragua Canal in the 1890's." *Americas* 20 (1964), 333-358.

312 Stansifer, Charles L. "E. George Squier and the Honduras Interoceanic Railroad Project." *Hispanic American Historical Review* 46 (1966), 1-27.

313 Williams, Mary W. *Anglo-American Isthmian Diplomacy, 1815-1915.* Washington, D.C.: American Historical Association, 1916.

TWENTIETH CENTURY (TO 1979)

Two major themes characterize United States policy toward Central America during this time period: (1) a condescending attitude toward the region's inhabitants; and (2) an effort to impose constitutional order, which meant establishment of political hegemony.

The first theme is most apparent in the two works by Dana G. Munro, who was assigned to the State Departments's Latin American Affairs Division during the early part of the twentieth century: *Intervention and Dollar Diplomacy* [entry 329] and *The United States and The Caribbean* [entry 330].

The second theme—the search for stability—is analyzed by Thomas M. Leonard's analysis of the 1923 Central American Conference [entry 325]. Raymond Buell's "The United States and Central American Stability, 1931" [entry 316] is a valuable contemporary study. Post-war military policy toward the region often has been charged with contributing to the maintenance of oligarchial governments. This is examined by Don L. Etchinson in *The United States and Militarism in Central America* [entry 321].

References to relations with individual countries can be found under the *National Histories* above: "Costa Rica," entries 90 through 92; "El Salvador," entries 123 through 128; "Guatemala," entries 173 through 193; "Honduras," entries 216 through 219; and "Nicaragua," entries 242, 243, and 253 through 265.

314 Alexander, Robert J. "United States and Central America." *Foreign Policy Bulletin* 4 (Jan. 1, 1961), 59-64.

315 Blasier, Cole. *The Hovering Giant: United States Responses to Revolutionary Change in Latin America 1910-1964.* Pittsburgh: University of Pittsburgh Press, 1976.

316 Buell, Raymond L. "The United States and Central American Stability." *Foreign Policy Reports* 7 (July 1931).

317 Challener, Richard D. *Admirals, Generals, and American Foreign Policy 1898-1914.* Princeton, NJ: Princeton University Press, 1973.

318 Clark, J. Reuben. *Memorandum on the Monroe Doctrine.* Washington, D.C.: G.P.O., 1930.

319 Crassweller, Robert D. *The Caribbean Community: Changing Societies and U.S. Policy.* New York: Praeger, 1972.

320 Davis, Harold E., and Larman C. Wilson, eds. *Latin American Foreign Policies: An Analysis 1810-1974.* Baltimore: Johns Hopkins University Press, 1975.

321 Etchison, Don L. *The United States and Militarism in Central America.* New York: Praeger, 1975.

322 Ferrell, Robert. "Repudiation of a Repudiation." *Journal of American History* 51 (Mar. 1965), 669-673.

323 Green, David. *The Containment of Latin America.* Chicago: Quandrangle, 1971.

324 Langley, Lester D. *The Banana Wars: An Inner History of American Empire, 1900-1934.* Lexington: University of Kentucky Press, 1983.

325 Leonard, Thomas M. *U. S. Policy and Arms Limitation in Central America: The Washington Conference of 1923.* Occasional Paper Series, No. 10. Center for the Study of Armament and Disarmament, California State University: Los Angeles, 1982.

326 Marlos, Salvador R. *Centro-America en el conflicto.* San Salvador: Cisneros, 1942.

327 Martz, John D. *Central America: The Crisis and the Challenge.* Chapel Hill: University of North Carolina Press, 1959.

328 Molineu, Harold. "The Concept of the Caribbean in the Latin American Policy of the United States." *Journal of Inter-American Studies and World Affairs* 15 (1973), 285-307.

329 Munro, Dana G. *Intervention and Dollar Diplomacy in the Caribbean, 1900-1921.* Princeton, NJ: Princeton University Press, 1974.

330 _____. *The United States and the Caribbean Republics 1921-33.* Princeton, NJ: Princeton University Press, 1974.

331 Neumann, William. *Recognition of Governments in the Americas.* Washington, D.C.: Foundation for Foreign Affairs, 1947.

332 Orantes, Isaac C. "The U.S. as a Regional Power in Central America." *Annals of International Studies* 2 (1971), 39-48.

333 Plank, John N. "The Caribbean: Intervention When and How." *Foreign Affairs* 44 (1965), 37-48.

334 Rippy, J. Fred. "State Department Operation: The Rama Road." *Inter-American Economic Affairs* 9 (Summer 1955), 17-32.

335 Scott, James Brown. "The Central American Peace Conference of 1907." *American Journal of International Law* 2 (Jan. 1908), 121-143.

336 Seidel, Robert N. *Progressive Pan Americanism 1906-1931.* Ithaca, NY: Cornell University Press, 1973.

337 Stansifer, Charles. "Application of the Tobar Doctrine to Central America." *The Americas* 23 (Jan. 1967), 251-272.

338 United States. Congress. House Committee on International Relations. Subcommittee on International Organizations. *Human Rights in Nicaragua, Guatemala and El Salvador: Implications for U.S. Policy.* 94th Congress, 2nd Session. Washington, D.C.: G.P.O., 1976.

339 "United States Strategies' for Central America." *NACLA's Latin America and Empire Report* 7 (May 1973), 1-40.

340 Welles, Summer. "Intervention and Interventions." *Foreign Affairs* 26 (1947), 116-133.

U. S. Investment, Trade and Imperialism

The broader question of U. S. economic imperialism is examined by Lloyd Gardner *Economic Aspects of New Deal Diplomacy* [entry 343] and Dick Steward *Trade and Hemisphere* [entry 351]. Indictments of the United and Standard Fruit Companies include the studies by Thomas L. Karnes, *Tropical Enterprises* [entry 344]; Charles D. Kepner, *Social Aspects of the Banana Industry* [entry 345]; and Thomas P. McCann, *An American Company* [entry 347]. Also see

U. S. Aid below [entries 360 through 364]; and entries 96 and 144 under EL SALVADOR and GUATEMALA above.

341 Brooks, Joseph J. "The Impact of U. S. Cotton Policy on Economic Development: The Cases of El Salvador and Nicaragua." *Public and International Affairs* 5 (1967), 191-214.

342 Clowand, Davis, Jr. *Schools in Banana Land.* Boston: United Fruit Company, 1965.

343 Gardner, Lloyd G. *Economic Aspects of New Deal Diplomacy.* Madison: University of Wisconsin Press, 1964.

344 Karnes, Thomas L. *Tropical Enterprises: The Standard Fruit and Steamship Company in Latin America.* Baton Rouge: Louisiana State University Press, 1978.

345 Kepner, Charles D. *Social Aspects of the Banana Industry.* New York: Columbia University Press, 1936.

346 May, Stacy and Galo Plaza. *The United Fruit Company in Latin America.* Washington, D.C.: National Planning Association, 1958.

347 McCann, Thomas P. *An American Company: The Tragedy of United Fruit.* New York: Crown, 1976.

348 Morrow, R. L. "A Conflict Between the Commercial Interests of the U. S. and its Foreign Policy." *Hispanic American Historical Review* 10 (Feb. 1930), 2-13.

349 Nearing, Scott and Joseph Freeman. *Dollar Diplomacy: A Study in American Imperialism.* New York: B. W. Huebsch & Viking Press, 1926.

350 Ponce, Reynolds. *La United Fruit Co. y la segunda república.* Comyaguela, Honduras: Bulnes, 1960.

351 Steward, Dick. *Trade and Hemisphere: The Good Neighbor Policy and Reciprocal Trade.* Columbia: University of Missouri Press, 1975.

352 United States. Department of Commerce. *Trade and Investment in Central America.* Washington, D.C.: G.P.O., 1965.

Policies of U.S. Presidents

The U. S. efforts to impose political stability on the region from 1900 to 1920 were reflected in the attitudes of Presidents Teddy Roosevelt and Woodrow Wilson. The studies by Selig Adler, John

M. Cooper and Frederick Marks describe presidential attitudes [entries 353, 354 and 357]. During the 1920s, the United States policy began to shift towards non-intervention. Alexander De Conde's study of Herbert Hoover [entry 355], and Franklin D. Roosevelt's essay [entry 358] describe the emerging U.S. attitude toward Latin America.

353 Adler, Selig. "Bryan and Wilsonian Caribbean Intervention." *Hispanic American Historical Review* 20 (1940), 198-226.

354 Cooper, John M. *The Warrior and the Priest: Woodrow Wilson and Theodore Roosevelt*, Cambridge, MA: Belknap Press, 1983.

355 De Conde, Alexander. *Herbert Hoover's Latin American Policy.* Stanford, CA: Stanford University Press, 1951.

356 Hill, Howard C. *Roosevelt and the Caribbean.* Chicago: University of Chicago Press, 1927.

357 Marks, Frederick W. *Velvet on Iron: The Diplomacy of Theodore Roosevelt*, Lincoln: University of Nebraska Press, 1979.

358 Roosevelt, Franklin D. "Our Foreign Policy: A Democratic View." *Foreign Affairs* 6 (July 1928).

359 Scholes, Walter V. and Marie V. Scholes. *The Foreign Policies of the Taft Administration.* Columbia: University of Missouri Press, 1970.

U. S. Aid

After 1960 the United States sought to improve economic conditions within the region, which in turn hopefully would alleviate the mass poverty. The 1963 Congressional Joint Economic Committee [entry 364] provides an excellent explanation of U. S. objectives. A major goal was to achieve regional economic integration. Also see *U. S. Investment and Trade* [entries 341 through 352] above. For U. S. policy regarding Central American economic integration see INTEGRATION AND UNION under **Central American History** particularly entries 40, 42, 43, 44 and 46.

360 McCamant, John F. *Development Assistance in Central America.* New York: Praeger, 1968.

361 Rice, E. B. *Extension in the Andes: An Evaluation of Official U.S. Assistance to Agricultural Extension Services in Central and South America.* Washington, D.C.: United States Agency for International Development, 1971.

362 Skidmore, William V. "Technical Assistance in Building Legal Infrastructure: Description of an Experimental AID Project in Central America." *The Journal of Developing Areas* 3 (July 1969), 549-566.

363 United States. Agency for International Development. Regional Office for Central America and Panama. *Economic Intergration Treaties of Central America.* Guatemala City: 1966.

364 United States. Congress. Joint Economic Committee. *Economic Policies and Programs in Middle America.* 88th Congress, 1st Session. Washington, D.C.: G.P.O.: 1963.

CONTEMPORARY CRISIS

Current U. S. foreign policy toward Central America cannot be isolated from internal regional affairs. Important references under **Central American History** include CONTEMPORARY CONFLICT, entries 19 through 34; EL SALVADOR, entries 102 through 122; HONDURAS, entries 216 through 219; and NICARAGUA, entries 255 through 265.

Ronald Reagan's military response to the crisis and the placing of it into the East-West Cold War struggle is explained by him [entry 375] and his Secretary of State George P. Shultz [entry 377]. A leading architect of Reagan's Latin American policy is UN Ambassador Jeane J. Kirkpatrick [entry 383]. Ambler Moss, Ambassador to Panama during the Carter administration, found great similarities in the goals and objectives of both Carter and Reagan toward Central America [entry 385]. Criticisms of Reagan's policy are presented by Democratic Senator Christopher Dodd [entry 366] and former Ambassador to El Salvador Robert White [entry 372].

Broader perspectives are found in entries 378 through 381; each is a collection of essays by specialists in U. S.—Caribbean relations. Also see *Communism and the Caribbean*, **Policy Recommendations**, and *Reagan's Caribbean Basin Initiative* below [entries 388 through 407].

Articles

365 Dinges, J. "Reagan and Revolution." *Progressive* 46 (May 1982), 22-26.

366 Dodd, Christopher J. "Democrats Response to Speech on Central America." *Vital Speeches of the Day* 49 (May 15, 1983), 454-456.

367 Enders, Thomas. "Building the Peace in Central America." *U.S. Department of State Bulletin* 82 (Oct. 1982), 1-7.

368 Farer, Thomas J. "Manage the Revolution?" *Foreign Policy* 52 (Fall 1983), 96-117.

369 Fuentes, Carlos. "Farewell, Monroe Doctrine." *Harpers* 263 (Aug. 1981), 29-35.

370 Gomer, Robert. "The United States and Central America." *Bulletin of the Atomic Scientist.* 39:7 (1983), 3-5.

371 Hayes, M. D. "The States in Central America and U.S. Policy Responses." *Current* 245 (Sept. 1982), 73-84.

372 Lowenthal, Abraham F. "Ronald Reagan and Latin America: Coping with Hegemony in Decline." In Kenneth Oye et.al., *Eagle Defiant: United States Foreign Policy in the 1980s.* Boston: Little Brown, 1983.

373 Millett, Richard. "The United States and Latin America." *Current History* 83 (Feb. 1984), 49-53+.

374 Nelson, A. "Central American Powder Keg, What Role for the United States." *Current* 228 (Dec. 1980), 34-43.

375 Reagan, Ronald. "The Problems in Central America." *Vital Speeches of the Day* 49 (May 15, 1983), 450-454.

376 Saxe-Fernandez, John. "The Central American Defense Council and Pax Americana." In Irving Louis Horowitz, Josue de Castro, and John Gerassi, eds. *Latin American Radicalism: A Documentary Report on Left and Nationalist Movements.* New York: Vintage, 1969, 75-101.

377 Shultz, George P. "Strengthening Democracy in Central America." *U.S. Department of State Bulletin* 83 (Apr. 1983), 37-45.

378 Smith, Wayne S. "U.S. Central American Policy: The Worst-Alternative Syndrome." *SAIS Review* 3:2 (1983), 6-13.

Books

379 Domínguez, Jorge I. *U.S. Interests and Policies in the Caribbean and Central America.* Washington, D.C.: American Enterprise Institute, 1982.

380 Erisman, Michael H. and John D. Martz, eds. *Collossus Challenged: The Struggle for Caribbean Influence.* Boulder Co.: Westview Press, 1982.

381 Fagen, Richard R. and Olga Pellicer, eds. *The Future of Central America: Policy Choices for the U.S. and Mexico.* Stanford: Stanford University Press, 1983.

382 Kirkpatrick, Jeane J. *Dictatorships and Doublestandards.* New York: Simon & Schuster, 1982.

383 Millett, Richard and W. Marvin Will, eds. *The Restless Caribbean: Changing Patterns of International Relations.* New York: Praeger, 1979.

384 Morris, Curtis S. *The United States-Caribbean Basin Military Connection: A Perspective on Regional Military to Military Relationships.* Washington, D.C.: American Enterprise Institute, 1983.

385 Moss, Ambler H. *Reflections of U.S. Policy Toward Central America: The Transition from Carter to Reagan.* Occasional Paper Series, Center for Advanced International Studies. Coral Gables, Florida: University of Miami, 1983.

386 Pearce, Jenny. *Under the Eagle: U.S. Intervention in Central America and the Caribbean.* Boston, MA: South End Press, 1983.

387 Wiarda, Howard J. and Janine T. Perfit. *Trade, Aid and U.S. Economic Policy in Latin America,* Washington, D.C.: American Enterprise Institute, 1983.

Communism in the Caribbean

The extent and meaning of communism in Central America is an important factor in understanding the contemporary crisis. Cole Blasier's *The Giant's Rival* and Jiri Valenta's essay [entries 388 and 394] are good starting points. The State Department's "White Paper," illustrates the Reagan administration's concern [entry 393]. Robert Wesson's work explains the meaning of communism within several selected Caribbean Basin countries [entries 395].

U. S. perceptions of communism in Central America following World War II are discussed in entry 7 under **Central American History** and under GUATEMALA, entries 184 through 193.

388 Blasier, Cole. *The Giant's Rival: The USSR and Latin America.* Pittsburgh: University of Pittsburgh Press, 1983.

389 Center for Strategic and International Studies. *Russia and the Caribbean.* Washington, D.C.: Georgetown University, 1973.

390 Chappell, William V. "Caribbean Sea: Another Russian Puddle." *Vital Speeches of the Day* 46 (Sept. 1, 1980), 689-691.

391 Flint, J. "More Cubas in the Making." *Forbes* 125 (Mar. 1980), 41-46+.

392 Ramet, Pedro and Fernando Lopez-Alves. "Moscow and the Revolutionary Left in Latin America." *Orbis* 28 (Summer 1984), 341-364.

393 "U.S. Policy in Central America." *The Stanley Foundation. U.S. Foreign Policy Report* (Oct. 1983), 48-59.

394 Valenta, Jiri. "The USSR, Cuba and the Crisis in Central America." *Orbis* 25 (Fall 1981), 715-746.

395 Wesson, Robert, ed. *Communism in Central America and the Caribbean.* Stanford: Hoover Institution Press, 1982.

Policy Recommendations

The continuing crisis in Central America, congressional debate over the CBI, and public debate over the course of U.S. action in the region contributed to Reagan's appointment of a National Commission, chaired by former Secretary of State Henry A. Kissinger, in August 1983. Its recommendations, issued in January 1984, recognized the deep rooted causes of the contemporary crisis, and called for increased military and economic programs [entry 399]. About the same time several other proposals by private groups appeared: *The Stanley Foundation Report* [entry 401]; *The Miami Report* [entry 402]; The Atlantic Council [entry 396]; and PACCA [entry 400]. The last, PACCA's "Changing Course" received most attention. It called for an end to U.S. support of the *contras*, normalization of relations with the Sandinistas, and a movement to achieve normal diplomatic and commercial relations with Cuba.

396 Atlantic Council of the United States. *Western Interests and U.S. Policy Options in the Caribbean Basin.* Washington, D.C.: Atlantic Council of the United States, 1983.

397 Bolin, William H. "Central America, Real Economic Help is Workable Now." *Foreign Affairs* 62 (Summer 1984), 1096-1106.

398 "Central American Relations/U.S. Policy Options." *Center Magazine* 17 (July/Aug. 1984), 15-37.

399 National Bipartisan Commission on Central America. *Report of the National Bipartisan Commission on Central America.* Washington, D.C.: G.P.O., 1984.

400 Policy Alternatives for the Caribbean and Central America. *Changing Course: Blueprint for Peace in Central America and the Caribbean.* Austin, TX: Central American Resource Center, 1984.

401 "U.S. Policy in Central America." *The Stanley Foundation. U.S. Foreign Policy Report* (Oct. 1983), 48-59.

402 University of Miami. Institute for International Studies. *The Miami Report: Recommendations on United States Policy Toward Latin America and the Caribbean.* Coral Gables: University of Miami, 1984.

Reagan's Caribbean Basin Initiative

Recognition of the need to meet the region's economic problems was the basis for the Caribbean Basin Initiative. An excellent summary of the program can be found in [entry 407]. An analysis of the initiative is the subject of the [entry 404].

403 "Background on the Caribbean Basin Initiative." *U.S. Department of State Bulletin* 82 (Apr. 1982), 7-32.

404 "The Caribbean Basin Intiative." [symposium] *Foreign Policy* 47 (Summer 1982), 114-138.

405 Dam, Kenneth W. "The Caribbean Basin Initiative and Central America." *U.S. Department of State Bulletin* 84 (Jan. 1984), 80-83.

406 Reagan, Ronald. "Caribbean Basin Initiative." *U.S. Department of State Bulletin* 82 (Apr. 1982), 1-7.

407 "The Reagan Caribbean Basin Initiative." *Congressional Digest* 62 (March 1983), 69-96.

Reference Works

Data on Central America in general and individual countries specifically are found in sources relating to Latin America as a whole. While this book concentrates on the major countries and largely excludes Belize (the former British Honduras) and Panama, several sources on them are included here because of these countries' relationships with their neighbors.

Overviews of a subject are particularly important for beginners doing research on Central America. The *Encyclopedia of Latin America* [entry 418] is a good place to start. It covers most aspects of Latin

American and Central American history, such as economics, politics, etc., including biography; also many of the articles provide bibliographic references. Similarly, the *Latin American Historical Dictionaries* series [entries 415, 421, 426, 435, 436 and 439] also provide solid introductions. These dictionaries focus on individual countries and provide brief definitions of selected topics, persons, events, geography, institutions, etc., usually with a short bibliography or bibliographic essay. The *Latin American Political Dictionary* [entry 443] provides definitions of concepts, institutions and events basic to the politics and economics of Latin America.

For more bibliographic sources, guides to the literature are useful. Some of the best and well-annotated ones are: Richard Dean Burns (ed.), *Guide to American Foreign Relations Since 1700* [entry 411], which contains much on Central America; John J. Finan and John Child, *Latin America: International Relations. A Guide to Information Sources* [entry 420], which includes data not only on Central America but also on the United States as it relates to the Inter-American System; and Charles C. Griffin, ed., *Latin America: A Guide to the Historical Literature* [entry 423], which is one of the most comprehensive guides to writings on Latin American history. This latter volume includes data on United States—Latin American relations as well as a chapter on international relations since 1830.

The *Handbook of Latin American Studies* [entry 475], an annual published since 1936, is the major source for current references in the fields of the social sciences and humanities. It contains extensive annotated bibliographies and bibliographic essays of current trends in each of the major disciplines covered.

There are several annuals or yearbooks which cover current political and social events of each Latin American country. The major one is *Latin America* [entry 419], which is a comprehensive annual survey of news developments, with much of the material originally having been published in *Facts-on-File*.   Indexes to periodicals or journal articles are necessary in order to locate pertinent current information. The specific one dealing with Latin America is *HAPI: Hispanic American Periodical Index* [entry 448], which is a detailed subject index to more than 200 major journals published in Latin Ameria and elsewhere. As of 1984 a new index, *HAPI: Hispanic American Periodical Index. Articles in English* [entry 451], covering 1976-1980 and a supplement for the years 1981-82, has indexed 113 journals and is the companion to the origional *HAPI.*

A more general periodical index is the Public Affairs Information Service *Bulletin* (commonly known as PAIS) [entry 441]. This is also a subject index to periodical articles, plus government documents, pamphlets and selected new books. It is published weekly with material from all English-speaking countries.

Broadcast news can also provide very up-to-date information. An unusual, and recent, index is the *Daily Report: Latin American Index. Foreign Broadcast Information Service* [entry 416]. This is a monthly index with material organized by both country and regional organizations.

Newspapers, of course, must be used for current information on political events. Indexes such as the *New York Times Index* will provide access to such information. However, *ISLA: Information Services on Latin America* [entry 428] provides the actual newspaper clippings. ISLA is published monthly, with a semi-annual index, which provides comprehensive coverage (by country) of Latin American political, economic and social news as published in eight major English-language newspapers.

Another type of index that should be used is the *Historical Abstracts* [entry 427] which contains abstracts of periodical articles, *festschriften* and other sources. These abstracts are published in two parts: Part A. *Modern History Abstracts* (1775-1914); and Part B: Twentieth Century Abstracts (1914-present). Although the selection of material is comprehensive, the *Handbook of Latin American Studies* is even more thorough. For those who do not read Spanish, it provides an English abstract of valuable articles and it indexes journals not covered by Latin American bibliographies, especially those concerned with current affairs.

There are many bibliographies which should be used, particularly for retrospective material. Most of those cited below focus on Central America, but a few have broader coverage. Only a few will be discussed here. Sidney D. Markham, *Colonial Central America: A Bibliography* [entry 433], which is annotated, is important because Colonial Central America is often overlooked. But many of today's problems are based upon events of this period.

Mario Rodrígues and Vicente C. Peloso, *A Guide for the Study of Culture in Central America* [entry 442] will provide sources for an understanding of Central American culture.

At the other extreme are two important bibliographies on revolutions and guerrilla movements in Latin America and including Central America. Martin H. Sable, *The Guerrilla Movement in Latin America since 1950: A Bibliography* [entry 444] covers the period 1950-1976. *Revolution and Structural Change in Latin America: A Bibliography on Ideology, Developtment and the Radical Left, 1930-1965* [entry 413], by Ronald H. Chilcote, is the definitive work on the subject.

The major and comprehensive guide to publications in English, Spanish and other languages in the field of United States—Latin American relations is Daniel F. Trask, et. al., *A Bibliography of United States—Latin American Relations since 1810: A Selected List of Eleven Thousand Published References* [entry 445]. This work has been updated by Michael C. Meyer in his *Supplement to A Bibliography of United States—Latin American Relations since 1810* [entry 430].

An important source for data that is usually hard to obtain is Arthur E. Groop, *A Bibliography of Latin American Bibliographies Published in Periodicals* [entry 424].

The *World Bibliography Series* has several books on individual countries, for Central America see *Belize, Guatemala, Nicaragua* and *Panama* [entries 450,422, 451, 432]. There is also one bibliography, not in the series, on British Honduras (1900-1970), now Belize, [entry 438].

Dissertations and theses are another resource that should not be overlooked. These unpublished works often contain bibliographies that would be of help to researchers. Some that concentrate on Latin America are: Carl W. Deal (ed.), *Latin America and the Caribbean: A Dissertation Bibliography* [entry 417]. The items listed are taken from the *Dissertation Abstracts International,* but without the abstracts, and cover the period 1962-1972. Harry A. Kantor, *A Bibliography of Unpublished Doctoral Dissertations and Masters Theses Dealing with the Governments, Politics and International Relations of Latin America* [entry 429] covers an earlier period, primarily 1940-1952, but some go back to 1911.

These reference works and other cited below will provide help to beginning researchers in the very complexed area of United States-Central American relations.

408 Araya Incera, Manuel E. *Materiales para la historia de las relaciones internacionales de Costa Rica: bibliografa,*fuentes impresas. San Pedro, Costa Rica: Centro de Investigaciones Históricas, Universidad de Costa Rica, 1980.

409 *Bibliography of the United States Marines in Nicaragua.* Washington, D. C.: Commandant of the U.S. Marine Corps, 1961.

410 Booth, John A. "Celebrating the Demise of Somocismo: Fifty Recent Spanish Sources on the Nicaragua Revolution." *Latin American Research Review* 17:1 (1982), 173-189.

411 Burns, Richard Dean, ed, *Guide to American Foreign Relations Since 1700.* Santa Barbara, CA: Clio, 1983.

412 California State University, Los Angeles. Latin American Studies Center. *Central America: A Bibliography.* 2nd ed. Los Angeles: CSULAS, Latin American Studies Center, 1980.

413 Chilcote, Ronald H. *Revolution and Structural Change in Latin America: A Bibliography on Ideology, Development and the Radical Left, 1930-1965.* 2 vols. Stanford, CA: Hoover Institution, 1970.

414 Cozen, Jon D., ed. *Latin America.* Washington, D. C.: Steyker-Post Publications, 1977.

415 Creedman, Thomas. *Historical Dictionary of Costa Rica.* Metuchen, NJ: Scarecrow Press, 1977. Latin American Historical Dictionaries, No. 16.

416 *Daily Report: Latin American Index. Foreign Broadcast Information Service.* New Canaan, CT: Newsbank, 1979-.

417 Deal, Carl W. *Latin America and the Caribbean: A Dissertation Bibliography.* Ann Arbor, MI: University Microfilms International, 1978.

418 Delpar, Helen, ed. *Encyclopedia of Latin America.* New York: McGraw-Hill, 1974.

419 Facts-on-File, Inc.   *Latin America.* New York: Facts-on-File, Inc., 1972.

420 Finan, John J. and John Child. *Latin America: International Relations. A Guide to Information Sources.* Detroit, MI: Gale, 1981.

421 Flemion, Philip F. *Historical Dictionary of El Salvador.* Metuchen, NJ: Scarecrow, 1972. Latin American Historical Dictionaries, No. 5.

422 Franklin, Woodman B. *Guatemala.* Santa Barbara: Clio, 1981. World Bibliography Series 9.

423 Griffin, Charles C., ed. *Latin America: A Guide to the Historical Literature.* Austin: University of Texas Press, 1971.

424 Gropp, Arthur E. *A Bibliography of Latin American Bibliographies Published in Periodicals.* 2 vols. Metuchen, NJ: Scarecrow, 1976.

425 *Handbook of Latin American Studies.* Gainesville: University of Florida Press, 1936-.

426 Hedrick, Basil C. and Anne K. Hedrick. *Historical Dictionary of Panama.* Metuchen, NJ: Scarecrow, 1970. Latin American Historical Dictionaries, No. 2.

427 *Historical Abstracts, 1775-1945.* vols. 1-16, 1955-1970. *Historical Abstracts.* Part A: *Modern History Abstracts, 1975-1914*; Part B: *Twentieth Century Abstracts, 1914-.* vol. 17, 1971-. Santa Barbara: American Bibliographic Center, 1955-.

428 *ISLA: Information Services on Latin America.* Orinda, CA: Informatin Services on Latin America, 1970-.

429 Kantor, Harry A. *Bibliography of José Figueres.* Tempe: Arizona State University, Center for Latin American Studies, 1972.

430 _____. *A Bibliography of Unpublished Doctoral Dissertations and Masters Theses Dealing with the Governments, Politics and International Relations of Latin America.* Gainesville, FL: Inter-American Bibliographical and Library Association, 1953.

431 Kruse, David S. *El Salvador Bibliography and Research Guide.* Cambridge, MA: Central America Information Office, 1982.

432 Langstaff, Eleanor De Selms, comp. *Panama.* Santa Barbara, CA: Clio, 1982. World Bibliographical Series 14.

433 Markham, Sidney D., comp. *Colonial Central America: A Bibliography.* Tempe: Arizona State University, Center for Latin American Studies, 1977.

434 Martinson, Tom L. *An Introductory Bibliography on Honduras.* Monticello, IL: Council of Planning Librarians, 1972.

435 Meyer, Harvey K. *Historical Dictionary of Honduras.* Metuchen, NJ: Scarecrow, 1976. Latin American Historical Dictionaries, No. 13.

436 _____. *Historical Dictionary of Nicaragua.* Metuchen, NJ: Scarecrow, 1972. Latin American Historical Dictionaries, No. 5.

437 Meyer, Michael C. *Supplement to A Bibliography of United States-Latin American Relations Since 1810.* Lincoln: University of Nebraska Press, 1979.

438 Minkel, Clarence W. and Richard H. Alderman. *A Bibliography of British Honduras (1900-1917).* East Lansing: Michigan State University, Latin American Studies Center, 1970.

439 Moore, Richard E. *Historical Dictionary of Guatemala.* Rev. ed. Metuchen, NJ: Scarecrow, 1973. Latin American Historical Dictionaries, No. 6.

440 Oqueli, Ramon. *Bibliografia sociopolitica de Honduras.* Tegucigalpa: Editorial Universitaria, 1981.

441 Public Affairs Information Service. *Bulletin.* New York: The Service, 1915-.

442 Rodrígues, Mario and Vincente C. Peloso. *A Guide for the Study of Culture in Central America.* Washington, D. C.: Pan American Union, 1968.

443 Rossi, Ernest E. and Jack C. Plano. *The Latin American Political Dictionary.* Santa Barbara: Clio, 1980.

444 Sable, Martin H. *The Guerrilla Movement in Latin America Since 1950: A Bibliography.* Milwaukee: University of Wisconsin, Center for Latin America, 1977.

445 Trask, David F., Michael C. Meyer, and Roger R. Trask, eds. *A Bibliography of United States-Latin American Relations Since 1810: A Selected List of Eleven Thousand Published References.* Lincoln: University of Nebraska Press, 1968.

446 United States. Department of the Army. *Latin America and the Caribbean: Analytic Survey of the Literature.* Rev. ed. Washington, D. C.: G.P.O., 1975.

447 United States. Library of Congress. Hispanic Division. *Human Rights in Latin America, 1964-1980. A Selective Annotated Bibliography.* Washington, D. C.: G.P.O., 1983.

448 Vagt, Barbara G., ed. *HAPI: Hispanic American Periodical Index.* Los Angeles: UCLA, Latin American Center, 1975-.

449 _____. *HAPI: Hispanic American Periodical Index. Articles in English, 1976-1980; Supplement, 1981-1982.* Los Angeles: UCLA, Latin American Center, and Faxon Press, 1984-.

450 Woodward, Ralph Lee, Jr. and Robert L. Collison, eds. *Belize.* Oxford, England: Clio, 1980. World Bibliographical Series 21.

451 _____. *Nicaragua.* Santa Barbara: Clio, 1983. World bibliographical Series 44.

AUTHOR INDEX

Taylor, Philip B., Jr., 191
Tierney, John J., Jr., 264
Tigner, James L., 275
Trask, David F., 445
Trask, Roger R., 445

U.S. Agency for International
    Development, 363
U.S. Congress, House, 128, 180,
    338
U.S. Congress, Joint Economic
    Committee, 364
U.S. Congress, Senate, 181
U.S. Dept. of Army, 182, 446
U.S. Dept. of Commerce, 352
U.S. Dept. of State, 192, 193, 265,
    276
U.S. Library of Congress, 447

Vagt, Barbara G., 448, 449
Valenta, Jiri, 394
Van Aken, Mark, 297
Van Alstyne, Richard W., 298, 299
Villeda Morales, Ramoin, 215
Vivas, Rafael Leivas, 200

Walker, Thomas W., 230, 245, 254
Wagner, C. Peter, 65
Weber, Henri, 253
Webre, Stephen, 109
Weiner, Peter H., 171
Welles, Sumner, 340
Wells, Henry, 86
Wesson, Robert, 395
Wheaton, Philip E., 218, 219
Whetten, Nathan, 135
White, Alastair, 95
White, Robert E., 122
Wiarda, Howard J., 387
Wilford, D. Sykes, 101
Wilford, Walton T., 101
Wilgus, A. Curtis, 16
Will, W. Marvin, 383

Williams, Mary W., 313
Wilson, Charles Marrow, 17
Wilson, Larman C., 320
Wionczek, Miguel S., 43
Woodward, Ralph Lee, Jr., 18, 172,
    183, 450, 451
Woosley, Lawrence H., 110
Wynia, Gary W., 56

Ydigoras Fuentes, Miguel, 143